THE GOOD, THE GREAT, AND THE UNFRIENDLY

ALA Editions purchases fund advocacy, awareness, and accreditation programs for library professionals worldwide.

THE GOOD, THE GREAT, AND THE *Unfriendly*

A Librarian's Guide to Working with Friends Groups

SALLY GARDNER REED | UNITED FOR LIBRARIES

An imprint of the American Library Association
Chicago 2017

SALLY GARDNER REED is the executive director of United for Libraries, a division of the American Library Association (ALA). United for Libraries provides support, education, and consultation to those groups affiliated with their local libraries to help increase and maximize their support—such as Friends, Trustees, and Foundation members—along with library directors who work with them. Prior to accepting this position in 2002, Reed spent nearly 20 years in library administration.

Reed is the author of nine books on library management, advocacy, volunteering, and fundraising, as well as numerous articles for professional library journals. She has presented programs and workshops to hundreds of Friends of Library groups, library boards, and librarian groups, nationally and internationally. Reed is the 2000 recipient of ALA's Herbert and Virginia White Award for promoting libraries and librarianship.

© 2017 by United for Libraries

Extensive effort has gone into ensuring the reliability of the information in this book; however, the publisher makes no warranty, express or implied, with respect to the material contained herein.

ISBNs
978-0-8389-1498-4 (paper)
978-0-8389-1522-6 (PDF)
978-0-8389-1523-3 (ePub)
978-0-8389-1524-0 (Kindle)

Library of Congress Cataloging-in-Publication Data

Names: Reed, Sally Gardner, 1953- author.
Title: The good, the great, and the unfriendly : a librarian's guide to working with friends groups / Sally Gardner Reed.
Description: Chicago : ALA Editions, an imprint of the American Library Association, 2017. Includes index.
Identifiers: LCCN 2016037885| ISBN 9780838914984 (pbk. : alk. paper) | ISBN 9780838915226 (pdf) | ISBN 9780838915233 (epub) | ISBN 9780838915240 (kindle)
Subjects: LCSH: Friends of the library—United States—Handbooks, manuals, etc. | Friends of the library—United States—Case studies.
Classification: LCC Z681.7.U5 R453 2017 | DDC 021.70973—dc23 LC record available at https://lccn.loc.gov/2016037885

Cover design by Kim Thornton. Image © Blan-k/Shutterstock, Inc. Interior design and composition by Dianne M. Rooney in Adobe Caslon Pro and ITC Novarese.

♾ This paper meets the requirements of ANSI/NISO Z39.48–1992 (Permanence of Paper).

Printed in the United States of America

21 20 19 18 17   5 4 3 2 1

*For Beth Nawalinski and Jillian Wentworth,
the best colleagues anyone could hope for!*

CONTENTS

Acknowledgments   ix

1. **How to Start a Friends Group (and Why You Should)**   *1*
2. **Engaging Active New (and Younger) Friends**   *23*
3. **Merging Friends and Foundations**   *37*
4. **Engaging Your Friends in Advocacy**   *49*
5. **When Friends Go Rogue**   *59*
6. **Ideas to Steal—Taking Your Friends from Good to Great**   *71*

APPENDIXES

- A   Sample Memorandum of Understanding   *133*
- B   Advocacy Campaigns: Legal Limits on Spending for Non-Profits   *135*
- C   Sponsorship and Gift Acceptance Policy   *137*
- D   Working Together: Roles and Responsibilities Guidelines   *140*
- E   Guidelines for Giving   *142*
- F   Making the Case for an Academic Friends of the Library Group   *144*
- G   Library Support for Friends Activities   *146*

Index   149

ACKNOWLEDGMENTS

With great appreciation to my colleague and friend Jillian Wentworth, who provided significant help in editing this book and getting it ready for publication.

How to Start a Friends Group (and Why You Should)

IF YOU'RE OLD ENOUGH, YOU'LL REMEMBER THE GOOD OL' DAYS WHEN library advocacy was not a part of the librarian's lexicon. There was a good reason for that: the typical library got a typical 4 percent or so increase every year to cover the typical rise in the cost of doing business. Back before the dawn of the digital era, libraries generally delivered a straightforward service; they bought, shelved, and circulated books and journals. They used their in-house resources to provide reference and information services and to provide services for youth. Oh, it's true, libraries diversified in the 1950s with filmstrips and again in the 1960s with phonographs, but basically, libraries both public and academic offered a single service operation. Easy peasy!

Then, everything changed. It all started with automated catalogs and circulation systems. There were both funders and patrons who lamented the loss of card catalogs and the ability to see from circulation cards who checked out books before them (never mind the invasion of privacy). Efficiency won out, however, and money was made available to make the move toward 21st century automation.

At about the same time, in the late 1980s and 1990s, libraries began taking steps to capture emerging digital resources to bring their promise for nearly unlimited access to information to their communities. The

Internet was clunky and mostly meant for academic purposes, but with acoustic couplers, it could be made available in public libraries as well. These were exciting times! Libraries were on the forefront of this new era, and many of us thought that this would give us amazing credibility with our funders. They would see us as the entrepreneurs that we truly were and fund libraries as the premier providers of online resources to the public. Boy, were we wrong!

In the public library world, funders initially told us to stick with books; academic libraries were luckier. In both cases, however, our world of information delivery was changed forever. Talk about diversification! Now libraries had many ways to deliver information and literature, and formats were (and are) constantly changing. Books do remain a stalwart, but we now have online information delivery as well. Some libraries continue to provide books on CD and movies on DVD, and who knows what's next. As diversified as format and content are, for a lot of libraries funding remains unresponsive to the costs of delivering widely diverse and constantly changing services that are in demand in the community and on campus. Enter a significant growth in fundraising for libraries, and that often means "friends" or foundations (more on that in chapter 3).

Via stand-alone databases as well as indexes and other information resources on floppy disk, academic libraries embraced technology well in advance of most but the largest public libraries. Because of the scholarly nature of academic libraries, it was easy to make the case to support the continuously changing technological environment. As networks evolved, however, the academic library as a "place" was occasionally questioned as access to digital resources could be achieved in dorm rooms, in the student union, in the cafeteria, and even across the globe.

As libraries progressed further into the digital age (thus, again, diversifying and increasing the costs of doing business significantly), public library funders looked around and decided that, as the Internet became ubiquitous, libraries had been rendered obsolete. After all, they told us, you can get anything on the Internet. Enter the age of advocacy. We had to help "educate" our funders about the fact that everything is *not* available on the Internet—at least not without a cost. And, hey, books are still circulating at a high rate.

Public library supporters had to reiterate the concern about the digital divide. Though this divide has become narrower, it has also become much, much deeper. There are those who do not have access to the Internet at home. Mostly, these are people living in or near poverty and who have the most to gain from access. Immediately, job search information that is almost entirely online comes to mind, but that's just one hurdle. Government information at national, state, and local levels is increasingly available only online. Those seeking information about health care services, social services, and food support services are at a decided disadvantage in getting access to the information that will help them and their families. Libraries are often the only point of Internet access for the "have-nots."

We continue to educate our funders that as we embrace all that technology has to offer, all types of libraries have become busier than ever before. It became important to let many of our funders know that even if they believe libraries are no longer essential, the community at large and the student body have been voting with their feet. Librarians have captured technology in its many forms and have turned their libraries into vibrant community and academic centers for learning of all types.

So, if your library doesn't have a "Friends of the Library" group (also known simply as "Friends"), here are some good reasons why it should.

The most obvious is for the fundraising. Friends—the good groups—raise money on a continual basis throughout the year and turn all that money right over to the library to help fill in the gaps that its annual budget doesn't cover.

But there is more that your group can do. A good Friends group can help you engage your community—academic or public. They can help you provide programming that helps your community understand the importance of the library on a daily basis. They can help your library reach out to underserved communities to let them know the library is there for them. And, importantly, they can let your funders know that the library is essential to the community and needs to be fully funded. Libraries across the country have seen their budgets increased or their cuts reversed because of the mighty efforts of their Friends groups (see chapter 4). You need Friends!

STARTING A PUBLIC LIBRARY FRIENDS GROUP

When it comes to starting a Friends group, as the saying goes, it's not rocket science! But, it does take some time from someone at the top. The library director or his or her designees, along with a trustee and an interested patron or two, are the best people to be in charge of getting this started.

Creating a Friends group will take some time, energy, and expertise. It's a good idea to do it right the first time rather than rush into it, make costly mistakes, and spend months or years to come trying to convince those who may have been turned off by a haphazard approach to join the Friends group once you do have your house in order.

Here are some of the issues that will have to be addressed as you start a new Friends group:

- Development of a core (executive) group of Friends members who will actually be doing most of the administrative work, recruiting of new members, and planning for Friends' activities.
- Development of a written operating agreement between Friends and library administration, outlining respective roles and authority (see appendix A).
- Establishment of purpose and determination of priorities for service.
- Development of an implementation structure that includes the leadership team and task forces for accomplishing the work for the year ahead, such as book sales, membership drive, fundraising events.
- Development of organizational bylaws and establishment as a 501(c)(3) organization for the purpose of accepting tax-deductible contributions.
- Development of a dues structure.
- Development of a recruitment campaign.

Addressing this list of objectives might seem daunting, but it constitutes important structural elements for a successful Friends groups. Taken one at a time, each of these components is readily achievable, and addressing each of them will ensure that your new group gets off on the right foot.

Development of a Core Group (Leadership Team)

A new Friends group will be established by a core group of library supporters who may well become the group's first leadership team. Because there is a good deal of up-front work to do before a membership campaign is kicked off, it makes sense that the work is shared among a small but hard-working group with a real desire to see success.

If you are a library administrator wanting to start a Friends group for your library, you would be wise to turn to those in your community or on campus who are known for their support of your library and for their ability to get things done. If you are a library patron or supporter who realizes that a Friends group can help the library increase and/or improve its services, let the library administrator know and ask him or her to join you (or a library staff liaison) in developing such a group.

Set up a meeting including five to ten supporters who are willing and able to bring a group to life. Go over the aforementioned list of objectives and begin to brainstorm how and who will accomplish them. Some of the objectives can be done simultaneously, and some will have to be done sequentially. For example, it's obvious that the core group will have to be established before a broad-based recruitment campaign begins. The list of objectives has been ordered in a relatively sequential way, and it might be best to tackle each in the order presented. For example, you won't be able to quality for 501(c)(3) status until you have first identified your organization's structure and developed your bylaws.

The most common way a new and somewhat taxing initiative fails is from lack of sustained momentum. That's why it's important to involve those people who you know will commit for the long term as members of the core committee. It's also important to schedule biweekly or monthly meetings until your core group is ready to launch its first membership campaign. What you are attempting to do is important; remember that and remind your group of that, so their level of commitment stays high.

The Formal Operating Agreement between the Friends and the Library

What? Do we really need to get it in writing? After all, the Friends and the library both have the same ultimate goal in mind—improving and enhancing the library's service. While it's true that you both are undoubtedly focused on the same goal, how that goal is best accomplished can be and often is the road to ruin for many Friends and libraries. The Friends, for example, might see early childhood learning as the most important public library service—and the library itself might even agree! However, that case may have been well made to the city administration and well funded, whereas the library's program budget may be non-existent and the library may be desperate to create programs for teenagers. Where will the Friends' money go? Should it go to picture books or teen programs? Who decides?

The academic library may be in serious need of a marketing campaign to raise its profile and cache on campus, but the Friends may have been most successful and most interested in raising money for new computers. Should the Friends continue down their traditional path that has been so successful or should they channel their resources into a new, professional marketing campaign? Again, who decides?

Nothing has doomed the relationship between Friends and the library more than misunderstandings about how the money and the time of the Friends group will be spent. Of course, the best working arrangement is to ensure that both the Friends and the library continue to keep one another in the loop. A member of the Friends' leadership team should always attend trustee or library governance meetings to keep this group up to date on the work of the Friends. Paradoxically, in public libraries, it is not recommended that a trustee be assigned to attend the Friends' meetings. Because the money raised is used for operational expenses, a trustee on the Friends board can get involved in decision-making that should be done at the management level, not the governance level.

Nothing will get the Friends and the library on the same page better than working together to design a plan of where the library is heading every year. What are the challenges ahead? What kinds of opportunities are out there that the Friends can help with? When this happens at the beginning of every fiscal year, the Friends' goals will be in alignment with those of the library, greatly reducing any conflicts about how resources will be employed.

To ensure that Friends and the library have a solid foundation for all future funding and advocacy initiatives, it's a good idea to work out how decisions regarding the Friends' efforts will be made and who will make them. The best (and most typical) practice is when the Friends provide funding for items on the library director's wish list. The ideal agreement will involve a spirit of mutual input into the final decision. In the end, the library administration has, by policy and position, the ultimate authority to accept or reject any gift to the library.

The goal in an operating agreement should be that all Friends' gifts (of money, time, or talent) meet exactly the highest needs of the library.

Considerations for the operating agreement should include answers to the following:

1. How will the Friends be incorporated into the library's planning process?
2. Are Friends authorized to spend their funds on organizations, agencies, programs, or projects that are not directly linked to the library and, if so, under what conditions? This will be included in the mission and bylaws of the Friends group, and it is good to be clear about this upfront, since money spent for other purposes can be a point of contention between the library and the Friends.
3. What support will the library give the Friends in terms of publicity, mailings, and/or labor for the book sale, space for the book sale, office space, office staff support, etc.?
4. Will the Friends engage in advocacy campaigns on behalf of the library and, if so, who will be involved in the design and message of those campaigns?
5. What role and authority will the Friends have for developing and implementing programs?

Establishing the Friends' Mission, Purpose, and Structure

Establishing a mission and articulating the purpose of your Friends group are excellent ways to focus your group on the roles you feel are most important, and they will help you develop a useful structure. In addition, knowing and articulating your key mission will help you recruit the people with the talents you need most to serve on committees, task forces, and in leadership roles. The purpose of your group will depend on the group's interests and the library's needs. If you are forming a Friends group for the first time, it is likely that there is some imminent need that you wish to address right away. This should be reflected in your mission, but the mission should not be so narrowly defined that once an immediate need is met, the mission of the Friends isn't as relevant to meeting future needs as it should be.

If you are establishing a Friends group because the library has been chronically under-funded to such a degree that services are inadequate and you want to form a group to pass a special tax levy or create an advocacy campaign aimed at the community or college administration, the role of advocates should be included in the mission. However, this role is best articulated generally, and there should be room for other enterprises. In other words, the group's mission might be to work to ensure adequate funds for the library through advocacy, fundraising, and promotion. Once you've been successful in achieving your initial objective (you've passed the levy or the administration has increased the library's budget), your group is now positioned to continue its good work in other ways—such as establishing a foundation, raising additional money for collections, or supporting a library marketing campaign. In general, most Friends groups work to achieve the following objectives:

- Provide direct additional financial assistance.
- Advocate for the library at the local level for increased financial support by the library's parent institution or the community.
- Encourage gifts.
- Raise money or pass bond issues for building and other capital projects.
- Provide volunteer services to the library.
- Increase community or campus awareness about the library.

The way in which any of these or other objectives are achieved will be determined by the group at large, along with input from the library's administration and governance. The most effective way to accomplish such goals is to set up a structure within the Friends organization so that focused work can be accomplished. Committees and/or task forces will be important for the smooth operation of the Friends group, and the successful achievement of its objectives include (but certainly aren't limited to):

- A leadership team
- Membership and Friends promotions
- Library promotions and advocacy
- Book sales
- Nominations
- Development
- Programs
- A newsletter

The charges for these committees and task forces will mostly be self-evident, but some might have charges that are a reflection of the library's needs. For example, the Development Task Force may want to work on establishing a fundraising campaign, a library foundation, or investigate further ways for the Friends to generate income. (Book sales are common ways to do this, but Friends groups across the country have been extremely creative in finding other ways.)

The leadership team will mostly oversee and support, as the work is assigned to a task force or is done by the library. It's entirely conceivable, for example, that the library staff will publish the newsletter under the Friends' name while the Friends contribute the funds and some of the content. The same is true for "Library Promotions and Advocacy." It may be that the trustees have this as their primary role, and the Friends' job will be to support their initiatives with resources, such as personnel and funds.

Establishment of Bylaws and 501(c)(3) Status

Before you go "live" with a membership drive, it's important to establish your Friends as a 501(c)(3) organization if this group is to work for a public library. If you are forming a group for an academic environment, you might be able to organize under the development office's status. For academics, it is not only wise but also imperative that your development office is on board with your plan to form a Friends group.

The 501(c)(3) status means that your organization is nonprofit and, therefore, tax exempt—which means your group can accept tax-deductible contributions. It's not that difficult to get this status, but in order to ensure that you cover your legal bases (on both the state and federal levels), it is best to hire an attorney, prevail upon your institution's attorney, or see if you can find an attorney within your library "family" and try to get pro bono assistance.

There will be some restrictions with the 501(c)(3) status such as a limit on advocacy. This doesn't mean you can't engage in capital campaigns or public awareness campaigns, but it does mean that you will be restricted as to how much of your group's income can be spent on "lobbying" (see appendix B). Much of what the Friends do in promoting the library, however, is "educational"—i.e., informing the community or administration about the value of libraries. Very often, an advocacy campaign will include much that is simply "educational" in nature; funds spent in this manner are completely legitimate.

One criterion that will be required for your 501(c)(3) status is that your organization has established bylaws. These bylaws should include:

1. Name of the Friends group and its headquarters (which might be the library itself).
2. Mission statement.
3. Who will be served by your organization?
4. Governing body, including:
   - Titles of officers.
   - Terms of office.
   - How officers are selected.
   - Appointment and duties of standing committees.
   - Provisions for special or ad hoc committees.
5. Meetings:
   - Time, place, and frequency of meetings.
   - Method for calling regular and special meetings.
   - Attendance requirements.
   - Quorum requirements.
   - Order of business.
6. Procedures for amending bylaws.
7. Parliamentary authority.
8. Dissolution clause (detailing what will happen to the group's assets if it should dissolve).
9. Date of adoption.

Be sure to check the requirements for your 501(c)(3) status before adopting your bylaws, as the IRS requires that certain items be included. To get an excellent overview of what will be required to establish your Friends as a nonprofit organization, go to www.nolo.com, and in the search window at the bottom of the lower left-hand side of the first web page, type in "nonprofit organizations." Next, click on "How to form a nonprofit organization." In addition to this excellent overview online, Nolo Press has a number of publications addressing the legal requirements for nonprofits.

GOING LIVE! BRINGING COMMUNITY INTO YOUR FRIENDS GROUP

Once you've completed all the groundwork involved in establishing a Friends group, it will be time to "grow" your group. Initially, you have probably worked with a fairly small core group of committed volunteers, but to ensure that your group is successful over the long haul, you'll want to include as many members of the library community and others who have a stake in the library's success as possible. You'll have to determine a number of things to wage an effective membership campaign. Among them will be:

- Dues
- Deliverables (what will members get in return)
- Membership approach and supporting materials such as brochures
- Promotion
- Follow-up

Dues and "Deliverables"

Before you start your membership campaign, you will have to figure out what you want your membership dues to be and what members will get in return—in other words, the "deliverables." This information will be incorporated into brochures and other membership promotional materials and dispersed via social media. What you ask for in dues and what you return as deliverables could well depend on the priorities of your organization. For example, if this Friends group is being developed to establish a strong and united voice to employ on behalf of the library's budget, you might want to start dues at $5. This way, everyone who wants to join can afford to do so, and you will get a lot more names in your database. If you offer several levels of membership, you will probably find that the vast majority of people join at the higher level, but again, you've ensured that all voices can be counted.

Obviously, if raising money is your goal, you might well want to start memberships at a much higher rate—say $35—and graduate the levels up to as much as $200 a year, if you think that is attainable. One effective way to persuade folks to join at higher levels is to graduate the benefits they will receive accordingly. For example, you might want to offer just receipt of the newsletter at the bottom level of membership, "First Night" tickets for the annual book sale for higher-level givers, and perhaps an invitation to an annual author event or formal dinner at the highest level.

Only you know what you are trying to accomplish, and only you can determine at what levels you are likely to strike a balance between ensuring broad-based participation and bringing in a fair amount of revenue—certainly at least enough revenue to cover the cost of membership benefits (including the newsletter).

In addition to annual membership dues, you might want to consider a "lifetime" membership, or in the case of a new group, a "founding" membership. This will help in two ways. First, the category option itself might inspire a potential member to make a significant gift towards your effort—more (start-up) money for your group. Second, you will know from the response you get to this option which members have both the wherewithal and the love of your cause to make a major gift. This is valuable information. Be sure to consider cultivating such members for future slots on your executive committee and for a role with the foundation, if your library has one or if your Friends group plans to establish one. Two tips on lifetime membership. First, be sure to make the cost for this category significant—$500 may sound like a lot of money today but it may become a paltry sum in ten years. Second, don't hesitate to send lifetime members a donor letter each year when you go out to other members for renewals—remember, high-level givers are letting you know that they have discretionary funds and that they like the library!

Membership Recruitment

You've done all your homework. You have an active and committed leadership team. You have established your mission and have worked with the library staff and trustees to develop an operating agreement. You are now a 501(c)(3) organization, or you are connected to your academic development office. You know how you want to structure the group, and you have determined what you will charge for membership. The time has come to bring on as many community members as possible. The membership campaign begins.

The most effective way to get members on board is to promote, promote, promote. Develop a brochure that is distributed at the front desk of the library and all its branches. Employ social media, and use every avenue available. Ensure that members can join online, and ensure that all promotions share how important membership contributions are to the library and, in a general way, how the money will be spent. If your group is typical, most new members will simply show their support by writing a check and want nothing more than to receive a monthly newsletter. If you include a check-off box for those who are willing to volunteer, many will see this as an opportunity for community engagement and will be delighted to become more actively involved. Those that do become actively engaged will evolve into a larger core group of Friends, from whom you will get most of your volunteer support and future officers. It's important to keep these more active new members engaged and nurtured.

Be sure you let your prospective members know what they will get for their membership. They will get a better library for one thing, and you should press that point home. Most people will welcome the opportunity to provide additional support to the library via the Friends and will want nothing more. Others will want the opportunity to be involved via committee assignment and ultimately a chance to be an officer. Many will look forward to a newsletter once a month to let them know what's new. Still others will be attracted to knowing ahead of time about library book sales and having an opportunity to attend a "sneak preview night." All of these are the "deliverables" that your core group has determined prior to the membership launch.

Work with the library staff to encourage them to give the brochure out to every patron at the checkout desk. If you are supporting an academic Friends group, work with your development office to see if there is a list of parents or alumni you can use to solicit membership from those who have a stake in the library, even if they aren't students. Be sure, as well, to solicit both membership and involvement among the faculty.

Think of places outside the library where you are likely to attract new members with your brochure. How about doctors' offices, grocery stores, the student center and cafeteria, or local bookstores? The brochure that you develop may be very simple and inexpensive at first. As time goes by and your membership grows, you might decide to make your promotional materials more polished with a Friends logo and a professionally designed layout. For now, however, the important thing is to get the opportunity for joining to as many outlets as possible.

Another good way to promote membership is to write a press release about the importance of library support through Friends. Make the press release compelling enough that it is likely to be published. Send it out through your social media avenues and to the local or campus paper. For example, start out with a proclamation that the new "Friends of Johnson

Library" are embarking on a community- or campus-wide membership campaign. Let the readers know why. What prompted you to start a Friends group in the first place? Was it a need for a better budget, a new building, more books and programs? Whatever caused your core group to establish a Friends group should be reiterated along with a strong pitch for the reason why it is so important. Be sure to include contact information, the range of dues members are asked to pay, and the opportunities members will have to become engaged in the organization.

Many Friends groups increase their membership ranks by hosting programs that will attract members of their community. An author program, for example, will no doubt be popular. Think about asking a local author to do a program on how to get published. If you provide the author with an opportunity to sell books and you promise lots of promotion about the program, you are likely to get a local writer to do it for free. Use this program (and all public programs your group sponsors) as an opportunity to promote membership in the Friends. Be sure you have a lot of brochures and encourage folks to join on the spot.

Be sure that everyone involved in the core group assists in extending your reach to members by promoting your Friends group at every opportunity. The members of your core group are likely involved in other civic or social organizations as are the trustees. Be sure they are asked to take a quantity of membership brochures to meetings of these groups. You can help motivate this core group by setting a challenge. Ask that each member of the executive board bring in a minimum of ten new members. After a defined length of time, honor that executive member who has brought in the most new members by taking her or him to lunch—the rest of you have to pay!

Let your imaginations go in deciding how you will encourage members in your new Friends group. With some ingenuity and a little work, you'll be surprised how many people in your community or on campus are willing to support the library through the Friends.

STARTING AN ACADEMIC FRIENDS GROUP

In addition to using some ideas from the guide to starting a public library Friends group, what follows is a guide written for academic Friends by Dr. Charles D. Hanson, Director of the Kettering University Library, used with permission.

Definition of "Friends of the Library"

What are Friends of the Library and what purpose do they serve in an academic library? What distinguishes a library Friends organization from other organizations on campus? I define Friends of the Library as an organization established to promote and financially support the resources, services, and needs of the academic library and to serve as advocates for the value of the library.

The Value of the Academic Library Friends Group

Library Friends have long played a vital role as a financial support group for public libraries. As academic libraries struggle to find financial support outside a formal budget process, the development of an academic library Friends group can be viewed as a positive strategy for many academic libraries. In fact, "direct financial support for library collections, services, and programs" topped the list of important benefits for an academic library in the survey conducted by the compilers of *Friends of College Libraries.*

The creation of an academic Friends group does have its challenges. Once cited as "the heart of an educational institution" by academic administrators, today's academic library is more often viewed as an academic department subject to the same demands for accountability, assessment, and outcomes as those of other academic departments. The current movement toward accountability in academia and proof of outcomes and evidence-based education means that academic libraries must often prove their value. Megan Oakleaf's *The Value of Academic Libraries* provides guidelines for library directors who want to demonstrate the value of academic libraries. If academic libraries are being asked to prove their worth, an academic Friends group can be a support group that demonstrates value.

Additional challenges cited in *Friends of College Libraries* include:

- Too much work for monetary return.
- Do not want to "compete" with other college development efforts or annual campaign.
- Lack of understanding of what a Friends group can and is doing.

All of these challenges can be dealt with if the academic library director is committed to the development of a Friends group. A commitment from the director is key to the sustainability of the Friends and defining the purpose of academic Friends, whether they will be advocates, social planners, fundraisers, volunteers, or public relations representatives for the library.

Here is one testimonial about the value of academic Friends:

> We have the best Friends! The Friends of the Mott Library volunteer their time and talents to promote the library, to host fun fundraising events, and to enhance library services. The Friends' Art Auction is one of their most successful and anticipated events, and they have also had success hosting silent auctions and Bingo games. Thanks to their hard work, Mott Library receives funds to host author visits, to purchase special collections, and to address unmet needs. Annually, our Friends provide funds to purchase popular reading materials as well as books to honor MCC retirees. In the past, they have picked up the costs of a new detection system, a remodel of the lobby entrance area, and preservation materials for the college archives. Our Friends' love of libraries is reflected in the good works they do for our library and our students! (Kathy Irwin, Director of Library Services, Mott Community College, Flint, Michigan)

The Purpose of the Friends

If Friends have great value for an academic library, what are some of the purposes a Friends group might serve? The Friends of the Kettering University Library and Archives (FOLA) work together for the following purpose:

> The purpose of the Friends shall be to promote an interest in the Library and Archives among students, faculty, staff, alumni, and public; to provide a fuller understanding of the role of the Library and Archives in education; to encourage gifts and bequests in support of the Library and Archives; and to assist the Kettering University Library and Archives in its educational mission through exhibits, programs, publications, and other means.

Expectations

It's always a good idea to be clear about what you expect to gain from your academic library Friends. At Kettering University, I expect my Friends to:

- Raise money to support the Library and Archives.
- Plan and support the speaker series, gaming nights, and special events for the Kettering University community and FOLA members.
- Host receptions to show appreciation for Kettering students, faculty, and staff.
- Together with library staff, organize the annual Book Sale and Silent Auction, including the member appreciation reception before the start of the book sale event.
- Recruit new members and provide names of possible FOLA Board members.
- Serve as goodwill ambassadors for the Library and Archives.

Developing an academic Friends group is all about building relationships and making connections. Expect a lot to get a lot in return.

Getting Started

Whether your goal is to start an academic library Friends group or revitalize a moribund Friends group, it is important to plan accordingly. Although it sounds simple to say, so much depends on library administration and the director's role in supporting the Friends and coordinating the activities of the Friends.

At Kettering University, I laid the groundwork for developing an academic Friends group by collaborating with University Advancement (aka the Development Office) in the planning and development of FOLA. I was fortunate to have a development officer who shared my enthusiasm for starting a Friends group, and he worked closely with me to write the bylaws, gather potential board members, and launch the organization. Some of the details of a nonprofit organization were also handled by University Advancement; for example, FOLA's 501(c)(3) status is under the umbrella of that office. University Advancement also assisted with the design for a FOLA membership brochure and for determination of membership fees. It's always a good idea to get the endorsement of the provost or university president in support of an academic Friends group.

And clearly, the academic Friends group will want to have most of the following fundamental structures to successfully manage the organization:

a. Bylaws
b. A board of directors (a core group of dedicated volunteers)
c. A membership brochure
d. Committees
e. A strategic plan (recommended)
f. Standard operating procedures (optional, but very useful as the organization evolves over time)
g. A website
h. A newsletter

Mission, Vision, and Values

It is important that the academic Friends' mission be closely aligned with the institutional mission and its emphasis on teaching and learning. Here are FOLA's mission, vision, and values statements.

MISSION STATEMENT

The mission of the Friends of the Kettering University Library and Archives (FOLA) is to advocate for the library and archives as vital centers of learning at Kettering University.

VISION STATEMENT

The Friends of the Kettering University Library and Archives (FOLA) is the key organization providing support, information, and advocacy for the Library & Archives to meet the demands of 21st century university education.

VALUES STATEMENT

In keeping with its mission FOLA adheres to the following values:

- Collaboration and networking
- Community service
- Advocacy
- Creativity

Marketing

Positive, successful stories about academic library Friends can be found in the United for Libraries newsletter, *The Voice for America's Libraries*, which contains a "Friends on Campus" section.

The *ACRL Standards for Libraries in Higher Education* has the following statements about performance indicators for external relations.

> **External Relations:** Libraries engage the campus and broader community through multiple strategies in order to advocate, educate, and promote their value.
>
> 9.1   The library contributes to external relations through communications, publications, events, and donor cultivation and stewardship.
>
> 9.2   The library communicates with the campus community regularly.
>
> 9.3   Library personnel convey a consistent message about the library and engage in their role as ambassadors in order to expand user awareness of resources, services, and expertise.

Social Capital

Communicate, communicate, communicate. A successful Friends group must maintain a system of communication with its immediate members as well as the entire campus community.

A Friends newsletter is one important communication method, but today it is increasingly important to communicate with "customers," however defined, through social media. It's easy to set up a Facebook or Twitter account for your academic Friends. However, "easy" does not necessarily translate into effective use of social media. As Laura Solomon has stated in her article in *American Libraries*, "Understanding Social Capital," one has to have a distinct audience of followers and be prepared to acknowledge comments and tweets posted on social media. Solomon maintains that social capital is "what allows any organization or individual to make requests of its followers successfully."

It's also possible to use e-blasts to get out the message about your Friends, their activities, and their fundraising. Jeannette Woodward in *Creating the Customer-Driven Academic Library* points out that "at the core of Library 2.0 is the belief that to prosper, libraries must partner with their customers to rethink the whole notion of the academic library." Building partnerships, fostering collaboration: that's what Friends are for.

TO BE OR NOT TO BE

When all is said and done, developing an academic Friends group requires ongoing support from library administration. The fact is, the library director/dean is the driving force behind the continuation of the Friends and the one primary factor leading to the success of the Friends. To be or not to be

---

TEN REASONS WHY YOU SHOULD HAVE AN ACADEMIC FRIENDS GROUP

What ultimately justifies the creation of an academic Friends group? Why are Friends important? Here are my ten reasons why an academic library might want a Friends group.

1. *Friends promote collaboration and cooperation.* Friends' activities and programs offer opportunities for collaborative planning with faculty, staff, and your surrounding community and local community organizations.
2. *Friends provide opportunities for networking.* Act local, think global. Friends can expand networking opportunities through participation with other local Friends groups and also state and national groups. For example, United for Libraries, the Friends (trustees, advocates, and foundations) division of the American Library Association, has excellent opportunities for getting involved in national library activities.
3. *Friends can assist with marketing and promoting your library.* Since the Friends work to support your library's services, they can adopt the library's service-oriented message as part of its message.
4. *Friends can offer opportunities for fundraising.* Friends have volunteers with talents and skills that can raise funds for those extra "dollops of library services" that your operating budget might not accommodate.

depends so much on energy, dedication, and enthusiasm for getting things accomplished. *You can do this!*

YOU GOTTA HAVE FRIENDS!

Friends groups all across the country are raising money and advocating for their libraries. In fact, many public libraries were started by women's groups that felt that their communities would be much improved if everyone had free access to reading and information—eventually these groups evolved

5. *Friends can lift you up when you are down.* Friends can be what the name implies: a Friend! Friends can share your concerns, help you when times are tough, provide a shoulder to cry on, and ease the burden.

6. *Friends can help you celebrate.* When was the last time you had a "Love Your Library" celebration in your library? Friends can assist with planning receptions, recognition events, and other celebrations. People love a reason to celebrate.

7. *Friends can speak (sometimes loudly) in support of your library.* Sometimes Friends speak quietly, by bringing in notable authors and writers at a speaker series, which keeps the library as a recognized participant in the academic community.

8. *Friends can maximize professional development and involvement.* Friends can help support library staff attendance at conferences and workshops and give recognition to outstanding achievement through the placement of honor books in the library.

9. *Friends can provide a sense of pride and accomplishment.* If you want your library to be a center of activity and a showcase of exemplary learning, the Friends can sometimes assist with special programs (e.g., "Gaming Night at the Library").

10. *The Friends' mission is strongly aligned with the academic library's mission.* The Friends volunteer their time in support of the library service mission and in support of the university's values and vision.

into what we call Friends of the Library groups today. Academic libraries have always been seen as central to their campus and learning, but Friends have been there to ensure that the library is prominent and raise extra money. It might surprise you to know that Harvard (then) College had the first known "Friends" group, which was formed in 1927!

Libraries are eager to use every avenue to engage with their communities. Friends groups are a strong link to making this happen. It seems true that behind every great library, there is (or soon will be!) a great Friends group.

Engaging Active New (and Younger) Friends

AS DAVID EISNER (CEO OF THE CORPORATION FOR NATIONAL AND COMmunity Service) said, "America's baby boomers are an untapped resource of extraordinary proportions. They are the largest, healthiest, best-educated generation in history—and they can leave an incredible legacy through service to others." But, a look around at today's public library Friends groups will too often reveal a group of (mainly) women "of a certain age." These groups are often concerned about what will happen to the group when they no longer participate in it. These groups are "aging out," and they don't know what to do about it. You can help your Friends group become more attractive to the emerging baby boomer volunteers.

The baby boomer generation has always gotten a lot of focus and press, and as this generation retires, the attention as to what they are doing and why continues. Reports are popping up everywhere that take a look at what retirement will mean for them. The findings from these studies are fascinating and have important ramifications for Friends. The most important finding is that the vast majority of newly retiring professionals and those nearing retirement are committed to giving back to their communities. In large numbers, they express a desire and willingness to volunteer in their communities. They are anxious to make a difference, so that makes them perfect potential Friends volunteers!

If your group is to take advantage of the new baby boomer retirees, it will be important to know what makes them tick. They are different than yesterday's volunteers. In the past, it was the stay-at-home moms who made up the core of America's volunteer workforce. These women who were raising their families had both time and inclination to also serve their communities. From school, to the hospital, to the library, these women helped make nonprofit organizations great.

Over time, however, more and more women began to enter the workforce along with raising their families. As this happened, they had less time to volunteer, and those who did often confined their efforts to where their children were—e.g., schools, Little Leagues, church youth programs, etc. The result? The women who made up the core of library Friends groups were seeing fewer and fewer recruits from the community. Again, I stress that this group has *primarily* been composed of women, but certainly not entirely.

There is a new group coming your way to help recruit the next generation of volunteers. It is composed of both men and women. They lead healthy and active lifestyles; many have been dedicated library users, and they are looking for opportunities to serve. There is one hitch, however: The *way* in which they want to serve is different. If your group is going to capture this opportunity, you will have to understand and adapt to their new perspectives and choices.

A SPECIAL NOTE ABOUT COLLEGE STUDENT VOLUNTEERS AND THE MILLENNIAL GENERATION

Everything that applies to the baby boomers is also true for millennials and those even younger. In fact, in 2015 this group was among the largest cohort of volunteers in America. There is a very good chance that changing the way your group does business will open the door for single-task opportunities for the younger crowd—in other words, students. Finite and one-day opportunities will make it easy for them. How about a day of painting the library's meeting room (with a pizza lunch) or a day of schlepping books for the annual book sale? What could be better than engaging and grooming them for Friends volunteer opportunities throughout their lives? Many young people are perfectly willing to commit to some volunteer time—but for a year? Probably not. For a weekend, you bet!

HOW TODAY'S VOLUNTEERS ARE DIFFERENT

Before your group makes an effort to attract baby boomer volunteers, it's important to understand how they are different and what they are looking for in the way of volunteer opportunities—and they are! So, just how are these new volunteers different? Following are characteristics that are common among them:

- They are better educated than their predecessors, and most will have worked full time prior to their volunteer service.
- They want to apply their skills and know-how in their volunteer work.
- They have traveled across the country and globe and will continue to do so.
- They want to see tangible results from their efforts.
- They will likely volunteer for a number of organizations—not just one.
- They want a great degree of flexibility in their volunteer schedule.
- They want to have input into how their work is accomplished.
- They are healthier than the last generation and want to stay active.
- They see volunteer work as a way to remain socially active.

This is a very good list of what they want, but studies and surveys show that there is definitely one thing they don't want: *They don't want to sit in meetings!* When you think about this new crop of volunteers coming from the professional world, it's really no surprise. They've been sitting in meetings all their work lives. Now, they want action!

When you consider the key components of what the new recruits are looking for—flexibility, tangible results, and the ability to have some input in what they are doing and how they do it, coupled with a lack of a desire to sit through monthly meetings—it's easy to see that for most Friends groups, things must change.

Here is what the typical Friends group currently looks like and how it operates: The Friends board is composed of the officers and the committee chairs. They meet once a month (perhaps skipping summers), and at their meetings, all the committee chairs report about what they are doing. The committee chairs are usually people who have been in those positions for a while—or have been recycled from past service on the board as an officer or from another committee.

The committees typically include membership, programs, book sale, nominations, newsletter, and publicity. The term "committee" is likely a misnomer, as all too often the chair actually is the committee and does most or all of the work. The book sale committee does pull in a number of volunteers out of necessity, but the chair is likely to have been in place for a long while, because after all, she or he has done it for so long that only she or he really knows how to run the sale.

Does this sound familiar to you? When you think about the work that a small group is doing, is it any wonder that Friends are having a hard time recruiting active new members? Some of the work that single Friends group members are doing can sometimes add up to a full-time job, and remember, newly retiring baby boomers are traveling and volunteering for a number of organizations—they are not looking for a new job! Oh, and did I say meetings?

When you look at the structure of your current Friends group, it should become increasingly clear that their set-up just won't be attractive to the majority of new volunteers. Sure, there will always be folks who love the library, have strong leadership qualities, and want to dedicate a good portion of their time in a leadership position with the Friends. That's great—you're going to need this person and a few more like him or her for your leadership team in a brand-new structure that will attract many, many volunteers and be a lot more fun for everyone. Read on.

HOW THE DIFFERENCES WILL AFFECT THE FUTURE OF FRIENDS GROUPS

Because Friends groups are typically structured with committees, and because many Friends groups are struggling to increase active participation in their group, it is probably time for your group to consider totally revamping how you do business.

A great way to help your Friends group "reimagine" the group to make it more attractive to new volunteers is to turn your board into a strategic planning leadership team! A planning retreat to take a fresh look at how your group operates can be both productive and fun.

Of course, before the Friends start rethinking their structure, you're all going to have to decide that you really *are* interested in making your group more attractive for those new volunteers who are retiring from the everyday workplace. They are looking around for opportunities to make a difference in their communities, and if your group doesn't provide an attractive opportunity for them, they will certainly go elsewhere. Remember, it's a competitive environment out there. Service organizations are all seeking talented volunteers, and those who adapt first will win!

If you are serious about raising the number of volunteers for the Friends, and if you really are interested in securing the future for your Friends group even as your current active members are "aging out," then it's time to embrace change. The good news is that the board can be the entity that designs that change! It's truly fun, and the end product, if you are successful, will be a Friends group ready and re-energized to support the library into the future.

So, let's go back and think about the characteristics of the "new" volunteers. They want results, they want flexibility, they want to apply their skills and abilities, and they want to have some input into how they accomplish the work that is needed. They might not want to come to meetings, but they are willing to work.

What this says can be summed up in two simple words: "task forces." Forget committees for the most part—especially forget committees of one! Think about all that your Friends do and all that you'd like to do during the course of the year, and consider all the steps it takes to accomplish those goals. Instead of a program committee, for example, think about looking at each program the Friends would like to present and what it will take—from conception to clean-up—to make one of those programs a success. Once that's done, you can create a task force to implement the process for that single program.

The irony is that with a structure based on a task force, the Friends will actually need *more* active volunteers than in the past. The good news is you can get them! When the leadership team breaks down all of its projects and efforts over the course of a year into easy-to-accomplish tasks, they'll be creating a structure that works perfectly with baby boomer volunteers. They will be asking for a limited amount of each volunteer's time, they will be involved in the process of accomplishing their task, they will see the results of their efforts, and they will work with others, providing them with a social as well as volunteer opportunity. See how well that matches with what volunteer professionals say they want?

NEW ROLES FOR THE LEADERSHIP TEAM

Just the simple step of thinking of the Friends board as a leadership team will help them begin to look at their yearlong efforts in a whole new way. Instead of boring meetings every month where everyone reports about what they're doing (yawn), they'll instead get to roll up their sleeves and imagine the year ahead. And even though studies show that the new generations of volunteers don't want to sit in meetings, they *can* attract those who are happy to attend "planning sessions"!

The Friends should think about turning every single board meeting into a strategic planning session. Instead of listening to reports, how about a full group discussion on what they want to accomplish during the year and how they're going to accomplish it? Consider starting your new year with the first big discussion—a discussion focused on how your leadership team can adapt to become more attractive to the next generation of volunteers.

Instead of thinking about committees, encourage your Friends to begin the planning process with a creative discussion about the goals for the coming year. What do they want to do? Raise money for the library, certainly. So how can that be done? Here are some typical programs Friends can engage in to raise money:

- Increasing membership
- Ticketed events
- Book sales
- Small-scale fundraisers

This is a good list for the year ahead and can provide great opportunities for teamwork and strategy discussions. When you break down each of the four programs listed, there is plenty of room for creativity. Taking a look at each goal area will give your Friends a place to start coming up with possible strategies and tactics. Just as an example, here's what they might come up with for increasing your group's membership:

Increasing Membership

- Public awareness campaign about Friends
- Social networking
- Website enhancements
- Letters to the editor
- Higher Friends visibility within library
- National Friends of Libraries Week activities
- Radio talk shows
- PSAs
- Recruiting new members
- Direct mail
- Online membership/credit card acceptance
- Each one reach one
- Brochure blitz at local community events

Breaking down each goal area into possible strategies will help your Friends to see that functioning as a leadership team will probably translate into higher impact for the library. It will also require lots of active members! What? Your Friends group is struggling to get a handful of active members, and now you are reading that to change the way your group operates, you're going to need more?

Yes, you are, and guess what? By looking at specific goals and projects for the coming year and brainstorming about ways to accomplish those goals, you will be setting up your group to become much more attractive to active new members. Members who want to engage in a project that has a beginning and an end. Members who want to see the results of their efforts, members who want to use their skills and socialize with others—sound familiar? You're right: We're talking about the baby boomer generation!

Once your Friends group has done the planning, they will be ready to recruit the task forces to help them accomplish their goals. The leadership team can recruit just one task force at a time to achieve its goals or several can be working at the same time, with the leadership team monitoring and supporting their efforts.

There are probably two main reasons that Friends groups aren't attracting active new members. The first is that they aren't asking—at least not aggressively and proactively. They will need to get on the phone, talk to their neighbors, and turn that incidental meeting with an acquaintance at the grocery store into a discussion about the exciting volunteer opportunities the group has to offer.

This leads to the second reason groups have trouble recruiting: They aren't specific about what they are asking. Who wants to become chair of the membership committee? What does that mean, what does one have to do, how long will the assignment last, will there be any help, and how much time will it take? These are all the questions a good potential volunteer will want to ask, and once he or she does, the answer will probably be "no," at least with members of the "new" volunteer force.

On the other hand, imagine a Friend is back on the phone, and instead of asking his or her friend to become chair of the membership committee (and perhaps its only member as well), the recruit is asked to join a special task force for publicizing Friends in advance of a membership recruitment campaign. Because the leadership team has done some strategic thinking of what that might entail, they can hand over some initial ideas, such as creating a social networking buzz, developing membership brochures, working with the local radio station to develop PSAs for Friends, and/or designing activities around National Friends of Libraries Week.

The leadership team should have a timeline in place and can let potential members of this task force know how long the campaign will last. The leadership team is armed with the information they need to tell a potential volunteer exactly what he or she is being asked to do. Are they asking this person to design a brochure, work with the printer, or distribute the brochure to outside agencies? Now they are asking a potential volunteer to engage in one discrete task within an exact time frame. If the leadership team does a little homework, they should be able to identify potential volunteers for the public awareness campaign who have worked or are currently working in marketing and promotion. That way, they can target volunteers who want to use their knowledge and expertise to give back to the community. Once they've pulled the team together, offered them whatever resources are available for the effort, and asked for reports to the leadership team on a regular basis (this can be done by email, phone, or even in person), you're ready to let them take it on. Perfect!

THE NUTS AND BOLTS OF WORKING WITH VOLUNTEER TASK FORCES

While you'll find that today's volunteers want to have control over their projects and a significant amount of authority to accomplish their work as they think best, they will absolutely still need guidance and support. It's important that every task force the leadership team creates has the following information:

- A specific end product or goal for their work. For example, the public awareness task force's goal should be to ensure that every member of the community knows about and appreciates the work of the Friends of the Library.
- A budget and resources available to them.
- Timeline—when the work should begin and finish.
- Background information that will help them. This will include information on what the Friends have done for the library over the course of the past year, and historically, how much money was raised last year and over time, what new materials and equipment were purchased, and how long the Friends group has been in existence.
- A list of ideas the leadership team has come up with to help the task force hit the ground running.
- Reporting requirements on project progress—to whom and how often.
- Name, physical address, phone number, and email address of their liaison to the leadership team.

Each task force will need a team leader. This probably sounds suspiciously like a committee chair, but because this work has a defined time frame for beginning and ending, the team leader position really is different from a traditional committee chair position. In the end, there does need to be someone responsible for bringing the group together virtually or in person, keeping track of what's being done by whom, and ensuring that progress continues until the goal is achieved.

It might be tempting for members of the "old guard"—e.g., the board—to take on team leader responsibilities for a task force, but it's best to avoid this if at all possible. First of all, someone who's been around for a while will very likely want to take control of the work of the task force. After all, the task force will no doubt come up with some wild and crazy ideas. Or, they may come up with strategies that the group has tried before that didn't work. It's just human nature for those who've shepherded a group along for a number of years to be resistant to letting go of the reins, and this could cause the loss of good ideas and good volunteers.

It might take some time, and it will definitely take some very proactive recruitment—especially in the beginning—but with a goal in hand and a long list of potential volunteers, your Friends group will be successful. Remember, there are a lot of folks out there just waiting to be asked. They might not even be regular library users, and perhaps they have never heard of the Friends before, but they'd still be happy to work on the behalf of the library.

Finding and Recruiting New Volunteers

A good, solid marketing campaign is a great way to enhance the Friends' attractiveness to potential volunteers and make them fully aware of what they do. Once your Friends have established some projects and goals they'd like to accomplish and have strategized about how these goals might be accomplished, they are much farther down the path to finding and recruiting volunteers than you ever were, with an open-ended invitation to chair a committee or run for office.

Couple this with a list of what support and guidance the leadership team can provide and what the timeline is, and they are well armed to be very specific in the kinds of volunteers needed and exactly what they'll be asking of them. The next step is determining how to reach them.

Technology has opened up ever-increasing channels for reaching out. Facebook, Twitter, Flickr, Pinterest, and other social media avenues (to show those photos of how much fun your Friends have), including a "join us" link on your web page that takes the website visitor to the various volunteer opportunities you have (specifying again the skills needed, the resources available, the timeline, and the goal), are all great ways to link up with people you don't even know.

Personal relationships are an excellent source of potential volunteers, and your group might want to start nurturing relationships with partners who can help you. Civic groups, religious organizations, senior centers, recreation centers, and other nonprofits are all possible resources. For academic libraries, think about engaging existing clubs, university support staff, and faculty. And don't forget the library staff! They will be able to connect the Friends with good patrons or those new to the community and possibly looking for social connections.

Again, having clear goals, timelines, skill requirements, and resources available will make members of the leadership team much more comfortable in reaching out to new volunteers. And, if they need a list of ideas, the Corporation for National and Community Service offers these suggestions:

For Public Libraries

Civic Organizations

    Fraternal organizations (e.g., Masons, Elks)

    Social organizations (e.g., Rotary, Kiwanis)

    Sororities and fraternities

    Religious organizations (e.g., B'inai B'rith, Knights of Columbus)

    Ethnic coalitions (e.g., African Cultural Association, 100 Black Men, Concerned Black Men)

Education-Based Institutions

    Adult education classes

    Lifelong learning programs

    Alumni organizations

Health Organizations

    Hospitals

    Hospice organizations

    Community clinics

    Doctor's offices

Work-Related Groups

    Pre-retirement workshops

    Businesses that allow time off for community service

    Professional associations

    Unions

    Chambers of commerce

Aging Advocacy Groups
>Professional retiree organizations (e.g., AARP)
>Senior centers or clubs

Senior Housing Organizations
>Retirement communities
>Assisted-living communities
>Age 50 and over active adult communities

Neighborhood/Community
>Neighborhood associations
>Local businesses
>Community festivals or fundraising events
>Bookstores and coffee shops
>Restaurants
>Grocery stores

For Academic Libraries

Campus Organizations/Students
>Academic clubs (e.g., chess, debate)
>Debate clubs
>Sororities and fraternities (which usually have a service requirement)

Faculty

Staff

Local Alumni

Academic Library Users

For public libraries, younger volunteers may be harder to find, but there are ways to track them down. Many high schools, for example, require their students to engage in some kind of community service. Getting in touch with the school administration is a good way to get started. They will let you know if their school has such a requirement and how you can publicize your opportunity. Even if the school doesn't have such a requirement, the administration will certainly help you connect with their student groups, such as the student council, sports teams, debate teams, and other groups whose members might be likely volunteers for a special project.

If you have a community college in town, you can also try to engage volunteers there—again going through the college's administration. Providing community service will be great for students' resumes, and you can pitch your volunteer opportunity this way. Whether a student plans to transition into a four-year college or directly enters the job market, having community service on his or her resume will give that student a leg up in a competitive environment.

Many city development offices or chambers of commerce have developed young people's social societies in order to help them connect with each other and to make staying in the city more attractive. These groups plan social events, but they also tend to volunteer. Finding out about them and ways to connect with them will pay off. A good place to start is probably through the chamber of commerce's offices.

Civic groups are doing everything they can to recruit the young professional. It's entirely likely someone in your group or on the library's staff belongs to one or more of these organizations. Make yourself known. Ask to be included in a future agenda for all these types of groups and make a pitch for volunteers. As always, offer a project opportunity—something of short duration with a beginning or an end. Because these groups include civic-minded people of all ages, you are likely to get new and continuing volunteers from them.

Don't forget about people you know. Maybe you don't personally know a young person, but you probably know someone who does. Just a handful of young people can help you not only recruit others, but they also can show you how to use social media for effective results. As with recruiting all volunteers, a proactive effort to reach out to them is key.

One of the most important jobs for someone on the leadership team is to keep a very accurate database for everyone who volunteers. You should include their names, their approximate ages, the jobs they did for you, and most importantly, their contact information. Everyone who has pitched in for a volunteer project has already signaled his or her willingness to help. Keep in touch with these volunteers, and ask them to volunteer again when new opportunities arise. Those who say "yes" again and again are likely to be perfect prospects for a future leadership team!

A PROFILE OF TODAY'S VOLUNTEERS

According to the Bureau of Labor Statistics for 2015, 35- to 44-year-olds and 45- to 54-year-olds were the most likely to volunteer (28.9 percent and 28 percent, respectively). Volunteer rates were lowest among 20- to 24-year-olds (18.4 percent). Teenagers (16- to 19-year-olds) continued to have a relatively high volunteer rate, at 26.4 percent. Over the year, the volunteer rates of those 55 and older were around 25 percent of the U.S. population (see www.bls.gov).

There are plenty of volunteers in every community and on every campus. The most important thing your leadership team or board can do for the future of your group is to take a good look at how your group is currently organized. Is the structure right for bringing in the 21st century volunteer? If not, take time to redesign and re-imagine your group. Try some new projects that might have appeal to students and the baby boomer generation, nurture your relationships, and then go get them!

Merging Friends and Foundations

FOR A VARIETY OF REASONS, SOME LIBRARY DIRECTORS DECIDE THAT IT would be better to merge a Friends group (or groups) with an existing foundation. It can be because the Friends aren't raising much money and/or are not active. Similarly, when the Friends are active and high functioning—raising lots of money and support for the library—working out any confusion between two or more fundraising groups can certainly be motivation as well. Usually, though, it is having a low-functioning Friends group that brings the idea of a merger to mind.

It can also be because the Friends are raising money but not giving much of it to the library (see chapter 5, "When Friends Go Rogue"). Some directors believe that with a singular money-raising support arm for the library, community donors will be less confused about whether they become Friends when they give money to the foundation, or that, since they've given to the Friends, the foundation shouldn't be coming back to them for more money. Some directors see that their wealthier neighborhood branches have terrific Friends groups, whereas the branches in the poorer neighborhoods have none. It's another case of the rich getting richer. A singular fundraising entity would allow financial resources to go to the branches most in need, as well as to wealthier neighborhood branches.

Following are two differing points of view on whether to maintain two separate organizations or whether to merge. Jane Rutledge is a member of a highly successful Friends group in Indiana, and Peter Pearson is the President and CEO of the Friends of the Saint Paul Public Library in Minnesota which, despite its name, acts as a foundation and raises hundreds of thousands of dollars each year for its library.

FRIENDS AND FOUNDATIONS, PART ONE

SEPARATE ORGANIZATIONS, SIMILAR GOALS

By Jane Rutledge,
Friends of Tippecanoe County (Ind.) Public Library

Our local library serves most of Tippecanoe County, Indiana, and is the home of a 44-year-old Friends group and a 12-year-old library foundation.

The Friends of the Tippecanoe County Public Library is a group whose core project is book sales. Four book sales a year, plus a thriving online sales project, bring in about 80 percent of our $100,000-plus budget, with the remainder of our income coming from membership dues and contributions. We budget $70,000 to $80,000 a year for library projects and try to keep our overhead at a minimum, so that we have some surplus most years, and we've been able to put aside funds for big projects.

We support all library programs—author visits, special speakers, children's programs, the summer reading club, and more. We annually award scholarships for staff members to continue their educations, and we pay for special continuing education programs for the library's staff day.

We try to fill in the gaps when special equipment or supplies are needed, and we fund staff recognition events, contribute generously to the staff social fund, and pay for the annual staff holiday dinner. We underwrite the publication of the library's newsletter.

Friends membership in recent years has hovered around the 650 mark. Fifteen years ago, when we began holding a members-only presale evening before each book sale, our membership increased dramatically,

---

Jane Rutledge has volunteered for Friends of the Library organizations for more than 30 years. She has served the Friends of Tippecanoe County Public Library in various positions (book sale chair, membership chair, president, and treasurer) and currently heads the online sales team. She has also served on the boards of Friends of Kansas Libraries, Friends of Indiana Libraries, and Friends of Libraries U.S.A.

and at about the same time, a major direct-mail membership campaign centered around a "Gold Card" membership level ($35 a year) brought in a large number of members who were generous donors.

Our basic membership remains at $10 a year, but about 40 percent of our members join at a better-than-basic level, and nearly 10 percent qualify for our "Benefactor Bookplate" level of $75 and above.

A thriving book sale project requires lots of volunteer labor, and we have been fortunate in recruiting a pool of 100 or more members who sign up for shifts at the book sales, sort books year-round, and help with other activities. Volunteers—whether they help once a year at a book sale or every week in the sorting room—constitute a committed group of library supporters.

When the library board decided to explore establishing a library foundation, they made the very wise decision to involve the Friends and build on the goodwill that the Friends had established through the years. The Foundation's creators looked upon the Friends as a complementary organization, with goals very similar to those of the Foundation and yet, with a very different focus.

The Friends group has specific funding goals and a book-sale-dependent budget, while the Foundation handles the "big asks," encourages planned giving and bequests, and works on grant applications. The Foundation has undertaken fund drives for furnishing our two new branch libraries, for two major renovations at our main library, and for establishing an endowment for future growth.

Friends officers were brought into the planning process very early and were a part of the discussions leading up to the Foundation's official founding. One piece of advice received early on—and followed—involved language. The Friends is a membership organization; the Foundation is not. The Foundation has donors but not members, and we have been careful to keep those functions clear and use the word "member" only in relationship to the Friends.

An important decision made in the early days involved the make-up of the Foundation's board of directors. The library's Board of Trustees appoints a member to serve on the Foundation board, and the Friends board also makes an appointment to the Foundation board. This has proved in practice to be a valuable means of coordination and cooperation, as all three boards are always aware of the activities of the others.

Another cooperative venture has been the Foundation's fundraising software. When the Foundation staff began looking for a software program, they invited the Friends membership chair to participate in their research and discussions, with the goal in mind of consolidating our mailing lists.

All of the Friends members were already on the mailing list for the library's newsletter, and a software program was chosen that enabled the Friends renewal and volunteer information to be added to the same database. This simplifies updating of address information, and the Foundation's administrative aide supplies the Friends with current mailing information and membership lists as needed.

Of course, consolidating the mailing information has added Friends members to the lists of prospects for the Foundation's fundraising efforts, and Friends members have been among the most generous individual donors to the Foundation's campaigns. Several of the large bequests that have come to the Foundation have been from people with long and strong relationships with the Friends.

The Friends of the Library as a group has also contributed to the Foundation's major campaigns. In appreciation, a children's activities room at one branch, an outdoor reading area at another, and a conference room at the main library now all bear the Friends name.

We're proud of our 12-year record of working together for the good of our county library. With the Friends continuing to develop community goodwill and personal commitments, as well as financing a range of library projects, and with the Foundation working to ensure sources of major funding for library improvements and expansion, we are a strong team making the future more secure for library services in Tippecanoe County.

FRIENDS AND FOUNDATIONS, PART TWO

IS A MERGED FRIENDS AND FOUNDATION RIGHT FOR YOUR LIBRARY?

By Peter Pearson, President and CEO,
The Friends of the Saint Paul (Minnesota) Public Library
and Director of Library Strategies Consulting Group

The library world is one of the few that I'm aware of in which there are two separate and distinct organizations that provide support for the same institution.

Peter Pearson has a master's degree in educational administration from the University of Minnesota. He has been a classroom teacher, school principal, and executive director of two nonprofit educational programs prior to taking this position as President of The Friends of the Saint Paul Public Library. Mr. Pearson currently sits on the Board of Directors of United for Libraries, a division of the American Library Association representing Friends, foundations, trustees, and advocates.

Library Friends groups have been in existence in many communities for more than 100 years. These venerable organizations have provided valuable service to their libraries, usually utilizing the skills of volunteers from the community who have a strong interest in books and libraries. The typical activities of a library Friends group can include book sales, author programs, advocacy, fundraising events, and volunteer activities within library buildings.

Library foundations, on the other hand, are a relatively new addition to the world of library support. The majority of library foundations have been formed within the last 20 years. Unlike their Friends counterparts, library foundations tend to be staff driven. Activities of library foundations tend to be higher-level fundraising, including annual fund solicitations from individuals for special programs and projects, planned giving activities, corporate foundation grant writing and sponsorships, capital campaign fundraising for new and renovated buildings, and major gift solicitation from individuals.

In many communities, these two different and distinct organizations operate side by side in support of the same library. Many times, the interaction between the two groups is very positive, and their work is complementary. However, there are times when having two separate nonprofit organizations supporting the same library can create some overlap in responsibilities and some confusion on the part of the community at large.

A model of support that is gaining in popularity is what I refer to as "the merged model" of a library Friends group and a library foundation. This merged model is the model that supports the Saint Paul Public Library in Minnesota, from which my experience arises. The activities of merged Friends and foundations include all of the activities of the two organizations separately. So, for instance, a merged library Friends and Foundation organization can conduct book sales, author programs, and advocacy activities, as well as all of the major fundraising activities, such as planned giving, major gifts, and capital campaign fundraising.

One of the keys to the success of a merged library Friends and foundation is a comprehensive committee structure, which allows individuals from the Friends and the foundation to engage in the activities for which they have the greatest passion. So, individuals who have a passion for used book sales would have an opportunity to pursue that activity, while individuals who prefer higher-level fundraising activities would find committee activities relevant to these interests also.

There are a number of advantages to the merged model of a library Friends group and foundation. Probably the most obvious advantage is that there is only one nonprofit organization that needs to recruit board members and file annual papers with the state and localities, thus reducing the administrative overhead needed to run two organizations.

A second strong advantage of the merged model is the time devoted by the library director and other key library staff in assisting the library support organizations. Library directors need to attend board meetings and committee meetings of their library support organizations, and having just one organization for this purpose can vastly reduce the amount of hours that library directors and staff spend in support of those organizations.

Another strength of the merged model is bringing together the two activities of advocacy and fundraising. These two activities are natural for all support organizations and can be done most effectively when one organization has private funds at its disposal to use as matching funds to leverage new public dollars being requested through advocacy efforts.

But probably the strongest reason for considering a merged organization is how the community at large might understand the library and its support structures. Most individuals who are not part of the insider group of library support people will have a difficult time understanding the distinction between a library Friends group and a library foundation. When we're looking to dramatically expand the number of people who make contributions to the library, the last thing we want to do is confuse these individuals with which organization does which activities. When a donor needs to ask, "Where do I write my check, to the Friends or the Foundation?" the likely answer may be that the donor will write it to neither. Having just one organization makes it very clear where an individual's financial and volunteer support will go.

Libraries that have developed the merged library Friends and foundation model typically note that these organizations are becoming extremely strong and vital, working closely with the library in all areas of interest to the library. And, being able to show excellent results in fundraising and advocacy efforts also attracts good board members to an organization.

Another reason that these organizations can be popular is that the mission is broad enough to appeal to almost anyone in the community. Organizations whose sole purpose is to sell used books or raise private funds might have a limited number of board members who are attracted to their missions. The merged organizations of library Friends and foundations can appeal to a broad cross section of every community.

The names associated with organizations that have merged a Friends group with a Foundation are always locally driven; no one format seems to apply to all libraries. In Saint Paul, the name of our organization has always been "The Friends of the Saint Paul Public Library." Locally, the name "Friends" carries a connotation of an organization with endowment funds and a track record of major fundraising and advocacy.

In San Francisco, which also has a merged model of Friends and foundation, the merged organization first took the name "the Friends and Foundation of the San Francisco Public Library," and then eventually went back to the name "Friends" in recent years. Again, these decisions are locally driven, and the name does not tend to have a major impact on the success of this model.

There appears to be more interest in the merged model now than I've seen at any time in the past. I have provided consulting to libraries across the country in this area, assessing the effectiveness of both organizations and helping libraries to determine whether or not a merged model is right for them. The important factors in deciding which way to go will be based on local needs and the history of each organization.

In any case, a change to a merged model should be done with a great deal of preliminary planning and the full involvement of both of the existing organizations to be certain that this is the right move for everyone involved. Even if a decision is made not to merge the two support groups, the process of discussing the issue certainly helps to clarify the roles and responsibilities of the existing Friends and the existing foundation. In these times of shrinking public resources, having efficient and effective library support organizations is more critical than ever.

THE DECISION IS MADE

Going forward with the decision to merge will no doubt bring to the forefront some significant challenges. It is typically the case that the idea for a merger comes from dissatisfaction with the Friends group or groups. If this is the case, it almost necessarily follows that these same groups will not make a merger easy. And they can certainly create significant roadblocks. There are few Friends and foundation mergers that were quick and easy. This is, in all likelihood, going to take a lot of time and patience.

Most Friends organizations have 501(c)(3) tax-exempt statuses. This means, among other things, they are really not "your" Friends group but a totally separate entity developed to raise money for the library. This is a good thing most of the time, because it means their money is protected from grabs by the city (if the library is a city or county department) or even grabs by ill-intentioned trustees who want to spend the money their way (this is, in fact, rare, but it does happen).

So, no executive decision by the library administration is going to work here. In fact, when a merger fails, it's almost always because the director tried to move too quickly or acted as though he or she had the authority to make the merger happen. In fact, because passionate people are involved, the best course of action is to move on this idea slowly and with all the key players at the table.

Many librarians who have successfully merged their groups report that ingratiating themselves on an individual basis with the people they'll later be trying to sway is critical. Whether you are the director or a foundation executive charged with making this happen, the very first step is to gain the trust of those who will be impacted. It's important to attend Friends meetings, attend programs, and volunteer to help in some way. Become a known and visible supporter of your Friends.

If you are dealing with unfriendly groups, that situation will have to be resolved before you even begin the work of bringing your Friends and foundation organizations together. It is not always easy to work out differences, but this must be done if you are to be successful and if you want to ensure that there is no lingering and public animus due to your efforts. Nothing will hurt your fundraising efforts in the future more than a public fight and a perception that the library doesn't appreciate what these sweet Friends have contributed to the library.

TIME TO BRING IN THE HIRED HELP

With rare exception, Friends groups tend to resist the idea to merge. It is even possible—and often is—that many of the groups' leaders will be angry. They might feel that they are underappreciated. They might feel that they are as important as any foundation—that they are the community's links to their neighborhood libraries. They love what they do—book sales, auctions, membership drives, and fundraising events—and they don't want to give up these activities. They will worry that the branch they have been supporting for many years will not get the extra financial support from the foundation that the Friends currently provide. These are all legitimate feelings and concerns.

In addition to legitimate concerns, you will also have to deal with a wide variety of personalities. If your Friends group is not high functioning, it is often due to one or a handful of members of the group's executive board who have taken over and have become bullies in running the group. These types of people will be extremely hard to convince.

You can soften any resistance before you even broach the topic of a merger. If the resistance is coming from the Friends, be sure to be their lead advocate. Write letters to the editor lauding their support, attend their meetings and programs, make a financial contribution, and share some of your staff and equipment with them. Become their best friend (if you aren't already).

The best way to begin discussions on the topic of a merger (after becoming their favorite Friends supporter) is often through a facilitated dialogue. If you expect some or much resistance, you should hire a library consultant who is well versed on the different roles of Friends and foundations and can guide the process toward understanding the positive aspects of merging for the library. Be sure to tip your hand before the consultant arrives. Though you'll get an unhappy response, don't spring the idea of a merger on your Friends and foundation when the consultant arrives. And this is key: While initial and even ongoing resistance may be based on individual wishes, in the end if a merger is being considered, it's because it's in the best interests of the library as a *whole*.

Everyone who has a stake in this proposition must be invited to the table (and everyone's schedule should be accommodated as far as you're possibly able). Friends leaders (current and former), branch managers, and foundation staff and board members should all have a chance to discuss the pros and cons of merging these two library support organizations.

A consultant will tease out from everyone the benefits of a merger as well as any possible pitfalls. Those who are highly resistant should have an opportunity to vent their concerns. It is critical that their work gets the respect it deserves. A good facilitator/consultant will manage the anger that is often accompanied by this idea.

Following is what the typical discussion will elicit:

PROS FOR MERGER	CONS FOR MERGER
There is no confusion within the community about who is raising money for the library—this is especially important during a capital campaign.	Local Friends of Libraries groups engage people at the local level—they are quintessentially "grassroots."
Only one 501(c)(3) is needed.	Friends can generate advocacy for their specific community via their membership rolls.
One entity will be handling the IRS 990 forms at the end of each year, reducing the opportunities for mistakes.	They allow everyone an opportunity to give to the library because memberships begin at a low price.
One reporting and acknowledgment system is in place.	
Successful foundations can raise hundreds of thousands of dollars a year for the library, whereas the Friends raise tens of thousands and not always for the library system as a whole (see community confusion above).	
The Foundation has paid staff who can ensure the future of the Foundation's work; many Friends groups are strictly voluntary.	
Members of the Friends group are aging out and long-term prospects look grim.	
The Friends volunteers who love working for the library can become library volunteers or sign up to work on Foundation campaigns and programs.	

KEEPING AT IT

Again, for most libraries, this is a long-term prospect. Friends who aren't on board with the idea of a merger might not be swayed by a consultant. But that's OK. At least now they have a better understanding of what's in it for the library and will have heard some compelling "pros."

It's important to keep the conversation alive. A potluck or wine and cheese event to talk about how the Friends might be engaged with the

> **TIPS FROM THOSE IN THE FIELD WHO'VE BEEN THERE, DONE THAT**
>
> In writing this chapter, I was helped by those in the field who have worked or are working to consolidate their foundations and Friends groups. I would like to thank Maria Stel, Executive Director of the Saint Helena, California, Public Library and Edward Warso, Director of the Geauga Public Library in Chardon, Ohio. Thanks also to Jeff Rubin, President of the Friends of the Sacramento, California, Public Library, who isn't involved in a merger but gave perspective from a very high-functioning Friends group. Following are their top tips from their experience:
>
> - Be a good supporter of both the Friends and foundation. Be present—be sure everyone knows you.
> - Start by finding ways the Friends and foundation can collaborate.
> - Be transparent in all efforts to merge.
> - Develop a thick skin; there is likely to be anger and frustration directed at you.
> - When there are branch library Friends, be sure to include the branch managers in your plans and your ongoing efforts.
> - Find Friends and foundation members who are in favor of the idea of merging, and lean on them to help you make the case.
> - Understand that this is likely to be a long-term project—be patient and stay the course.

foundation is a good start. The food and drink help to turn a meeting that might be tense into a much more relaxed atmosphere. During the event, the director and foundation executive should talk about ways in which the foundation and Friends can help each other to reduce redundancies.

Many foundations are willing to use their (typically) more sophisticated accounting and acknowledgement software to record and keep track of Friends members. Friends, in turn, could share their membership databases with the foundation to increase their number of potential prospects for large gifts.

Working to find fun and important ways for the foundation and Friends to collaborate will help move you further in the direction of the merger. If you have more than one Friends group, you can let them continue "aging out" and asking branch managers not to encourage new members (though you can't stop the Friends from doing so). If you have a single system-wide Friends group, they may age out or you may finally convince them to support the merger.

It will be critically important as you keep the dialogue open that you find as many ways to engage members of the Friends group to participate in the foundation's efforts. The more connected the Friends group becomes to the foundation, the more they'll soften to the idea of merging. In fact, foundation members and staff may find a person or persons on the Friends group who "gets it" about merging and can be your ambassador to the rest of the Friends.

Engaging Your Friends in Advocacy

AS GREAT AS FRIENDS CAN BE IN RAISING MONEY FOR YOUR LIBRARY, THEY can be even more valuable in raising their voices. Look at it this way: The Friends might give you $50,000 each year, but if they can get a budget increase for the library, they will be giving you a lot more money. This is money that (typically) becomes the new budget foundation for next year—it's a gift that just keeps on giving.

Very often (and certainly in the academic environment), it's the Friends and the trustees who take the reins in an advocacy campaign when the library director is an "at-will" employee of the city or town. In these cases, the library director can and should be a visible member of the community at large—always extolling the relevance, value, and the essential nature of the library to the people it serves. Being a visible promoter and educator about the library will give a lot of credibility to the campaign.

But it shouldn't fall to the library director to be the sole advocate of an increasing budget, a fight for new facilities, or a battle against budget cuts. And as mentioned, some library directors would be seen as insubordinate to their direct supervisors if they were the "face" of the campaign (except in the case where the director reports to a governing board).

Whether or not a library director can be directly involved in advocacy, any efforts are exponential when many people who are not seen as having a conflict of interest support a cause—pay raises, for example. The library belongs to its community, and its community should be raising its collective voice starting with your closest support groups!

ACADEMIC LIBRARY FRIENDS AND ADVOCACY

Though academic libraries will likely not engage in a public advocacy campaign, the members of the Friends group can be tremendous advocates to support the library's financial goals. They can write letters to the editor of the school's news media; they can request time of the academic radio station to say why they support the library and why the library needs more money, a new building, an updated technological infrastructure, or whatever the case may be. They can make calls to the decision-makers and use whatever influence they wield on the library's behalf. Some of the ideas below may work for academic campaigns, but person to person and a presence on various forms of media (actual and digital) often works best.

PUBLIC LIBRARY FRIENDS AND ADVOCACY

When you're ready to develop an advocacy plan, talk to your Friends board and see if they and their more active members would be willing to work with you on developing this plan. If the Friends are engaged in the beginning, they are much more likely to stay engaged and be willing to engage others in the implementation of the plan. In addition, bringing in your Friends at the beginning will likely ensure that they will finance the plan to the highest degree possible by IRS rules. (See appendix B.) A working group of 10 to 15 is all you need for plan development; a crew of hundreds should be recruited for implementation of the various tasks that will be required.

Here's what the planning team will need to determine (in relatively sequential order):

- Timeline—when will the campaign need to culminate to be successful?
- Campaign slogan and developing talking points.

- The budget available for the campaign.
- Types of strategies that will be involved.
- Who will be in charge of each strategy?
- The number of volunteers needed to carry out the strategies.
- The time frames for implementation of each strategy.
- Celebrating success!

TIMELINE

This seems simple, but the start of your efforts is not when the community funders invite public input into the planned budget. You might have some success with a last-minute rally at the hearing, but it will likely be far less than you are hoping for. As the librarian, you know when the initial decisions are being made and what the likely plans are for the library's budget. If you suspect or were told that your budget will have to be cut or level funded, this is the time to begin the campaign. If you wait until the final draft, those who worked on the budget will be unhappy to see it challenged. A lot of work has gone into it, and they will have to find other areas to cut if they raise the library's budget. Let your Friends (and foundation members and trustees) start making their voices heard as soon as you know your budget is in trouble.

CAMPAIGN SLOGAN

A strong, short, to the point slogan will tie all your activities together. In addition, a logo will tell everyone who sees it that this is a library advocacy campaign at a glance. A well-developed slogan and logo should be included in all your visual efforts. It can be hard to come up with the perfect phrase and that can become doubly hard when lots of people are "wordsmithing" it. On the other hand, creativity seems to play a strong hand during brainstorming sessions.

Looking at what other campaigns have done can help you develop your own marketing slogan. Here are a few that have been used in recent years:

- Open Doors Unlock Potential—Dallas, Texas
- 1% for Libraries—Norfolk, Virginia (when the library's budget was less than 1 percent of the city's overall operating budget)

- When does $1.00 get you $10.87? When you vote YES for the Wood Library—Canandaigua, New York
- Libraries Yes! Invest in Success!—Josephine Community Libraries, Grants Pass, Oregon
- Opening Doors, Opening Minds—Cleveland Heights, Ohio
- Keep Columbus Metropolitan Library Strong—Columbus, Ohio
- Save Our Library—Many campaigns across the country

In addition to the slogan, the campaign should have about ten talking points. These will be used by Friends and other volunteers as they write letters to the editor, speak to the Lions Club, and talk to their neighbors and friends. In short, these talking points should ensure that everyone stays on message. Typical talking points include:

> Over 70 million Americans used their local public library for digital access in 2012. We need the hours, computers, trained staff, and up-to-date technology infrastructure to accommodate the many residents of our city and county who have no access to the Internet at home or work.
>
> The Digital Divide has narrowed but has become much deeper. In today's world, those without access are left far behind in getting government (including local government) information. Job seekers are now dependent on access to find employment, children and teens doing homework fall behind, as they can't compete with students who have home access to the Internet, and seniors need access to health and Medicare information.
>
> According to the National Association for the Education of Young Children (NAEYC), there is a 30-million-word gap between children entering kindergarten with a book-rich experience and those who have not had such an opportunity—and many never catch up. Our library has a rich collection of books for young children and their parents, but we don't have the staff to engage in the aggressive outreach services to reach children at risk in our community.
>
> In our community, 43 percent of our residents have not acquired a high school diploma by age 25. School students who don't have home resources such as Internet access, quiet study

spaces, or parents who can help with homework are at a very serious disadvantage for completion of homework. Staffed and resourced appropriately, our library can provide excellent in-house and outreach services to help kids at risk.

Teens are susceptible to becoming involved in gangs, vandalism, and crime when they have nothing better to do. Our library provides an alternative place for teens—and libraries are fun! Engaging teens in the library requires staff reaching out to schools and the community about what resources we have to offer that will be meaningful to them. We do not have the budget necessary for these kinds of outreach services.

THE CAMPAIGN BUDGET

Depending on the type of campaign you are planning, the Friends may well be able to fund the entire thing. When "lobbying" for the library, there is a legal limit as to how much a 501(c)(3) can spend (see appendix B). However, much of your campaign will include educating your funders about why libraries matter, and many of the strategies won't cost anything—like developing a speakers' bureau and writing letters to the editor.

If, however, you plan to go full tilt, your Friends might want to develop a separate 501(c)(4) organization. These groups are allowed to participate in politics, so long as politics do not become their primary focus. What that means in practice is that Friends must spend less than 50 percent of their money on politics. So long as they don't run afoul of that threshold, the groups can influence elections, which they typically do through advertising.

Friends can donate money to the 501(c)(4) but only to the limit described for grassroots lobbying in appendix B. The 501(c)(4) can, however, solicit grants and donations, and in doing this, they will also be making the case for the library and why the campaign is so important—a double benefit!

CAMPAIGN STRATEGIES

Once again, the Friends can be extremely helpful and effective in this area. While the planning committee does not have to be very large (and ideally it includes several Friends members), implementing strategies will (and should) require many, many hands on deck. In fact, the more people that become involved, the more your campaign is likely to be successful.

When you look at typical strategies, it will be clear that Friends with their vast membership database (you shouldn't look to just the "active" Friends members but at their entire roster) have access to the numbers of volunteers needed to wage a successful campaign. If asked to perform one discreet task—such as writing a letter to the editor, spending a couple of hours getting petitions signed, or placing a yard sign in their yard—you will find that many otherwise "checkbook" members will be most willing.

Designing strategies to get your message out isn't complicated; in fact, most are just common sense. The following is a list of ideas that can be easily employed. The more people you involve, the easier implementation will be, and the more successful your campaign will be.

> *Flyers*—Be sure to incorporate a slogan and logo. The flyers should explain what you are asking the community to do and, importantly, why it matters. What difference will it make to the library, and what, in turn, will the library be able to do for the community? A very small group of people can put this flyer together, triple check it for accuracy, and get them printed up. The Friends and people recruited for this task can ensure that the flyers are distributed all around town, to other businesses and organizations friendly to your cause. Flyers are a good way to penetrate the community with your message. Be sure they are eye catching and ubiquitous.
>
> *Yard signs*—A very common and simple way to encourage people who see them to take the action you desire. For example: "Vote 'Yes' for the library" or "Call the Mayor and tell her you support the library" (with the official phone number included).
>
> *Buttons*—Another simple and cost-effective way to let people know that the wearers support the library's campaign. Though everyone involved should start implementing strategies, the final plan may be attendance at the budget hearing *en masse*, all wearing the buttons.
>
> *Meeting with newspaper editorial board and local news stations*—It's important to let the editorial board of your local paper (yes, I did say "paper"!) and the local news departments of your

television stations know about your campaign. Explain what you're asking for and why it is so important for the library and ultimately the community. It would be great to get their endorsement, but in meeting with them, you'll be showing that you respect that they have a need to know and this will certainly garner some if not all of their favor. Take the board president, the foundation president, and the Friends president with you. These representatives can discuss the ways in which they are supporting the campaign.

Letters to the editor—Your team has developed a good set of talking points; you can put them to good use by asking members of the community and your known support groups (e.g., your Friends!) to write letters to the editor using the talking points to buttress what they want to say, only in their own words. For example, members of the Friends can say why they support the library to the degree that they donate money and time to help assure its success. The trustees can deliver the message about why this campaign is so important.

Radio and television Public Service Announcements (PSAs)—If you have a community television station, you might get time to present a public service announcement, and the staff of the station may be willing to help you produce it. Local radio stations are really great places to place PSAs. Be sure to pay the station manager a visit and see what he or she can do for you. Depending on your town or city's size, the station manager may be willing to do this for free and even help develop and produce the PSAs. In larger cities, it is likely that you'll have to pay for airtime, but the station(s) may be willing to give you a discount. If you have a local community college or university with a broadcasting curriculum, you may be able to get a student to develop and produce the PSAs so they are polished. People listen to the radio in their cars all the time—nowadays, probably more often than they watch conventional television!

Newspaper advertisements—Whether you are asking the public to "Vote Yes" or to call their council representative or mayor, sometimes taking out a paid ad is the best way to get your message out to the people. Friends and/or foundations, once again, may be able and willing to spend their money on such an ad. It should be timed to coincide with when the action will have the most effect. In a "vote yes" campaign, the day before the ballot box opens would probably be best. For example, if asking the public to contact the local decision makers about a budget increase, just as the funders get started with the budget would be best. The ad should clearly state that it is paid for by the Friends and/or foundation of the library.

Speakers' bureau—Here's another area where you will want outside voices to be speaking out for the library. Using the talking points you've developed, Friends and foundation members can be asked to speak to civic and cultural organizations willing to listen. It's important when deploying a speakers' bureau that the speakers understand the talking points and know that at the end of their presentation they must "close the deal" by telling the audience exactly what you'd like them to do: "Vote yes," for example, or "Write letters to the editor," or "Call the mayor." This is a wonderful opportunity to expand your support base in a meaningful way. If possible, it should also be an opportunity to pass around a sign-up sheet for others who would like to volunteer for the campaign.

Digital presence—Most Friends groups and foundations have a strong digital media presence such as newsletters that are sent out by email, robust Facebook presences, the use of Twitter, Instagram, Snapchat and other forms of engaging their members. Friends should feel completely unapologetic in using every form of communication available to tell their members about the campaign—why it's important and what library supporters can do to help.

THE NUTS AND BOLTS OF IMPLEMENTATION

For every strategy you employ, there should be a person in charge. This volunteer should understand how much money is available for the strategy, when the strategy needs to be completed to be effective, and how many people will be necessary to carry it out.

Staying on top of things is critical for success. This doesn't (usually) involve solving complex problems, but it does mean that everyone who has volunteered or has been drafted knows exactly what they are to do, when they are to do it, and what the budget limits are if there is money involved.

Looking at the strategies, you will see that they all involve a finite beginning and end. The advocacy planning team should check in with the strategy leader at the beginning, middle, and end of the task to ensure that the implementation is going according to plan.

YOUR FRIENDS CAN (AND SHOULD) ADVOCATE!

Some groups feel that they are not allowed to "lobby" on behalf of the library, but that's just nonsense. It's probably the most important activity they can engage in. Be sure to work with them, so they fully understand their legal limits of lobbying and remind them that much of what is required in an advocacy campaign is educational in nature and, therefore, not part of the calculation the IRS uses for advocacy or lobbying (see appendix B).

Most importantly, the Friends should know how critical their involvement is in an advocacy campaign. Their voices have huge credibility. They are already spending their time, energy, and creativity to raise money for the library. They have nothing to gain from a better-funded library except a better library, and that's what they will be building for the community when they speak out and engage.

When Friends Go Rogue

IF YOU BOUGHT THIS BOOK AND WENT STRAIGHT TO THIS CHAPTER, I feel your pain! Luckily, most Friends groups are absolutely essential to the library; not only do they raise money for the library, they can also be ambassadors for the library, promoting its value throughout the community. They can provide tremendous help in a capital campaign (in fact, many Friends groups were established as a result of people coming together to help fundraise for a major building or technology project). The best Friends groups will contribute to the morale of you and your staff by being fond supporters of all you do.

But sometimes, Friends groups become quite unfriendly, and when this happens, it can be a terrible strain on your relations with them, it can deprive your library of much needed money, it can cause morale to drop, and it can cause a loss of sleep and worry over what to do. Almost always, the rift comes from personalities that make working out a functional relationship with them (or him or her) more an art than a science.

Because Friends groups are typically 501(c)(3) organizations, they are a totally separate entity from the library, and technically, you have no jurisdiction over them (although they can be restricted from using your name in the fundraising efforts if they are not helping the library—more on this later). This can make working with an unfriendly group even more difficult but not impossible! This chapter will address the most common types of problems libraries and librarians face with dysfunctional Friends, which include the following:

- Friends are secretive and unwilling to share their organizational and financial information with the library.
- Friends don't invite the library's administration to their meetings.
- Friends believe that, because they raise the money, they should decide how it is spent.
- Friends are withholding money for which the library has a legitimate need.
- Friends are opposing library policy and/or direction.
- Friends are giving their money to organizations or initiatives outside the library.
- Friends have become "clubish" and follow their own agenda versus that of their mission.
- Friends' officers don't turn over, and they begin to think of the money raised as their own.

SECRETIVE FRIENDS WHO DON'T WANT YOU AT THEIR MEETINGS

Many librarians believe that they are entitled to access Friends' documents and that Friends meetings must be open to the public. Sadly, bylaws are not public documents unless your state has nonprofit governing laws stating otherwise, and your state's open-meeting laws might not apply to nonprofits (they usually refer only to government agencies, which, of course, Friends groups aren't). This means that, when you ask for their records and their minutes or even ask to attend their meetings, they might have the right to refuse. One piece of information that is available to you (and might yield the information you need) is their 990 forms, which they have to file with the IRS every year to protect their nonprofit status. You can find your group's filings at https://projects.propublica.org/nonprofits or at www.guidestar.org.

How did it come to this? There could be a variety of reasons: Perhaps the previous director alienated the Friends, and they have decided that in the future, they will keep the work to themselves to avoid any more unpleasantness. It could be that some of the Friends have decided that this is *their* group and that the library has too much influence on their decision-making—which is nonsense because they exist to serve the *library's* needs. Or—maybe they just don't like you!

So, what can you do? It's time to become their best Friend! Join them and make a membership donation. If they have open membership meetings, attend. Hold a potluck to thank them for all they've done for the library. Write an op-ed thanking them for the gifts they've made in the past. Try to personally befriend a member of their board who would be willing to be your spokesperson for more transparency. Ask them what more you can do to help their efforts.

If you have faced a brick wall in trying to get information from them, you should stop trying immediately and swallow your pride. It will take time (and hopefully a change in their leadership) for you to worm your way into their hearts, but if you can do so, you'll have gone a long way in improving relationships for the long term.

FRIENDS TO LIBRARY: "IT'S OUR MONEY, WE'LL DECIDE HOW IT'S SPENT!"

OK, first of all, it's not really their money. They don't own it; they are stewards of it. But, try telling them that! Obviously, all gifts to the library should have final approval from the director or in the case of larger gifts, often the approval of the trustees. For a sample gift acceptance policy, see appendix C.

It's important for the Friends to realize that the library director is the one who knows what the library needs most. The Friends might want that marble bench outside the library (with their name inscribed on it), but the library director knows that what's really needed at this point are new laptops in the teen center. It's clearly a sad misuse of funds if the Friends get their way and an important need of the library goes wanting. For a chart of roles for Friends, directors, and trustees, see appendix D.

So how do you resolve this issue? You can start by including them in your short-term planning. Once a year, when your budget is being set for the following year, ask for time on the Friends' agenda to share with them what the year ahead is looking like. (If you are anticipating budget cuts—this is also a great time to rally them for advocacy.) Discuss with your group the community trends that will impact library services. Do you have a population of people who are Vietnamese moving in? What will that mean for collection development and community programs? Are new families moving in, raising the number of children you'll be serving, and how will this impact youth services?

Explore the goals you have for the coming year with your Friends, and discuss how they can ensure that their contributions align with these goals. Let them have a chance to give input as well. This type of respectful once-a-year dialogue will help put you on the same page, and when you go to them for money for a new Vietnamese collection, they'll likely have the check waiting for you!

Bad things happen in a vacuum. It's important to include the Friends as you survey the year ahead and continue to keep them in the loop throughout the year. Be sure to have a gift acceptance policy in place so that when you say no to the marble bench, you have an objective policy to back you up. And finally, present the Friends with a wish list, so that rather than using their own imaginations about what the library needs most, they'll have a menu of items that *you* know are most needed.

FRIENDS HOLDING ONTO THE MONEY THEY'VE RAISED

The first of two of the most common calls we get at United for Libraries is from Friends who say, "We never see the library director until she needs something. She treats us like an open checkbook and rarely even thanks us for what we do." The second call comes from library directors who lament, "The Friends are sitting on thousands of dollars that they say they are saving for a rainy day. It's pouring outside! How can I get them to release their funds?"

This scenario is a twist on Friends deciding how their money will be spent. It comes from a misunderstanding of what the library needs and why. As is always the case, communication is critical here. The problem once again is that Friends are breaching good faith with donors who believe that their money will be spent to help the library, rather than sitting in a bank account somewhere.

The best Friends groups (if they are not acting as a foundation whose role is to amass great amounts of money for future library projects) spend nearly everything they make each year on the library (see appendix E). This annual spending provides the catalyst for fundraising in the following year. When the Friends have a close-to-zero balance in their checkbook, it creates an urgency for more fundraising.

So, how do you ask your Friends to give even more? This is a sensitive area because if they are giving *some* money each year, you could come across as ungrateful or, worse yet, greedy. I know, I know—this is not for you but for the library! If you don't even know how much the Friends have, that creates an even trickier problem—how much do you ask for to convince them to dig into their nest egg? Again, you can find their financial information from guidestar.org.

Once you know how much money they're holding onto, the next step is to develop a plan for your library of important services, facilities support, new collections, technology start-ups, and/or anything else you believe your library needs *right now!* If you don't want your Friends to pick piecemeal from your plan, you should tie it into one project; for example, if you don't already have a "makerspace" in your library, you could ask your Friends to provide the technology you need for such as space as a start-up. Most Friends (rightly) don't want to spend their money on items for which the funding authority should be paying as part of the library's basic services.

Another way to encourage the Friends to let go of that rainy-day fund is to ask for the money as a catalyst for future fundraising or library construction. Asking for the funds to engage a fundraising consultant or a building consultant is an excellent way to leverage their money into a big project and for them to be leaders at the beginning.

Excellent relations and communications are critical here as in all your relationships with your Friends. You might include with the types of requests already mentioned a discussion of how your Friends see themselves as supporting the library. You can let them know that best practices among the country's Friends groups are to spend most of their money each year so that when they go out to raise money in subsequent years, they have much more to boast about in terms of what they've recently sponsored. It will make the case for repeat donations, as well as for recruiting new donors/members. Show them the Fact Sheet (appendix E) from the national Friends organization. Sometimes (sad but true), it takes an outside organization to make the same points you've been making for others to finally listen.

FRIENDS PUBLICLY OPPOSING LIBRARY POLICY AND/OR DIRECTION

It's true—some library Friends groups actually go out publicly to oppose the library policies and decisions. For example, there was once a California Friends group that started an active campaign to oppose the library's building plans. Incredible, right? The library board of trustees had received a perfect parcel of land (for free!) upon which to build a new central library. It was right in the geographic middle of the city's population growth (and projected growth according to the city's planning and zoning department).

The new location, however, meant a one- to two-mile drive from where the central library was currently located, which was basically in the old village of this bustling and growing city. The Friends leadership at the time also lived in the old village; they liked the convenience of getting to their library relatively quickly, and they worried about the building's future. So, in their own self-interest, they began making buttons, attending council meetings, passing petitions, and writing letters to the editor, making it clear that the Friends of the Library opposed the new building site.

We do live in a democracy, and one of our most cherished rights is freedom of speech. So, it's certainly OK to form a "Citizens Against the Library" group and oppose the plans under that moniker. It is *not* OK to use the Friends designation for this activity. Not only is it highly unethical, but it's most likely in violation of their bylaws as well, most of which include *supporting* the library in their mission statement and, therefore, could threaten their 501(c)(3) status.

Another similar but even more dastardly scenario happened a few years back. A Maryland city was in financial straits and, in an effort to consolidate resources, planned to close some underused neighborhood branches. I don't have to tell you, this did not go well with the neighborhoods targeted! So what happened? The Friends (the good guys) held their annual membership meeting to elect new officers. What did the angry citizens do? They began joining the Friends in legion numbers; then, they attended the membership meeting and wrote in their own candidates for the board. They staged a coup!

It worked, and once the new "Friends" board was installed, they immediately began to oppose the closings with their "Friends of the Library" designation. It was a brilliant plan, and as with the aforementioned case, it was an easier sell to the public—"Gee, even the Friends of the Library are opposed."

It is unlikely that a group this unfriendly would be amendable to your requests that they not use the Friends designation. You can point out that this puts the Friends' 501(c)(3) designation in jeopardy, but they are not likely to care because they have another agenda entirely. If you can't get these folks to back down willingly, you'll probably want to end your association with them entirely (see "Getting a Divorce from Your Friends" later in this chapter).

FRIENDS OF THE LIBRARY SUPPORTING OTHER ORGANIZATIONS

It is most typically the case that the Friends bylaws reflect a singular purpose of supporting the library. Some, though, have included the phrase "the library and literacy" in their mission statement. If literacy is included, that opens the door for them to support other compatible but not directly related organizations in addition to or even instead of the library.

Partnerships for literacy are so very important, and that means it requires all hands on deck. The appalling rate of illiteracy and semi-literacy in America can certainly be viewed as the number one threat to our country. In an increasingly global and technical world, we simply will be unable to compete if we can't ensure that our children are successful in school. We know that targeting early childhood literacy is especially important.

As the library director, your job is to be involved or at least quite knowledgeable about the Friends' work with other literacy agencies, and you should highly encourage your Friends to work with library staff in creating meaningful partnerships for literacy and to fund those. If they call themselves "Friends of the Library," there should be library input, agreement, and involvement with literacy partnerships. If the balance tips to an organization that diminishes in any significant way their direct support for your library, you should discuss this with them. Perhaps they can reform as "Friends of Literacy," leaving the Friends of the Library title available so that you can start a new group.

Other than literacy (and then only if you agree and it's a part of their mission), the Friends should not spend their money on other groups and organizations. Again, it's a breach of faith with their donors/members who believe they are supporting the *library* when they support the Friends, and it's likely outside of their mission. What to do? If you are unable to convince them to support only what they have nonprofit status to support (i.e., what's in their bylaws), see "Getting a Divorce from Your Friends" later in this chapter.

IT'S OUR CLUB: DO YOU KNOW THE SECRET HANDSHAKE?

This is a fairly typical problem, and it can certainly contribute to the scenarios already mentioned. The group was founded years ago, and over time, the same five to ten (sometimes even less) people run it. They might do the usual things—like having a membership drive (for contributions only), holding a used book sale, maybe sponsoring a program or two, and supporting the summer reading and learning program.

This would be OK, except the group is aging out, and though you hear them complain that "they just can't seem to recruit new and younger members," they certainly aren't trying very hard to do so. They are very content with the group they have. They are very content with the work they do (and have done for ages). They circulate among the board positions—"Betty" serving as president this year and board member-at-large the next—and finally returning to the president's position once again. They don't hold membership meetings, and they don't try new things.

If you, too, are content with the group as is, maybe this isn't a problem for you—for now. The truth is, however, that we all age out eventually, and if the Friends aren't bringing in new members, the group could go away entirely in several years, leaving you to have to do the harder work of starting a new Friends group all over again (see chapter 1).

In addition, a cliquish Friends group is not engaging community in their group—a positive activity in its own right. They may even be sending out negative vibes (even unintentionally) that others are unwelcome in their group, and this could certainly impact their fundraising ability. Finally, most groups that don't grow and evolve over time fail to take on new initiatives and think differently about how they're structured and how they can raise even more money for the library. If the active group is small and ingrown, their ability to be strong advocates when you need them is hindered—they may not even be willing to advocate at all if it's not something "they've always done."

How can you convince them to open the doors to active new members? As with many of the remedies, you should be their strongest supporter. You should ingratiate yourself with them, and let them know how much you appreciate their work. You can let them know that they have created a strong legacy for the library that you are worried won't succeed them. You would hate to see all their wonderful efforts on behalf of the library diminished by not having succession planning in the mix of all they do. Let them know you are most willing to help with the recruiting effort.

Some groups become so small and clannish that they aren't raising the kind of money you know is out there. The problem is, because they are carrying the Friends of the Library title, you're hard pressed to start a new fundraising and support organization. What would you call this new group? How could this be done without confusing your community?

Once again, the answer may be that you have to let this Friends group go. If they are standing in the way of creating a robust grassroots fundraising environment for the library, they really aren't your "Friends." If you can't get them to change and grow, it might be time for the last unhappy step.

GETTING A DIVORCE FROM YOUR FRIENDS

The time has come. You've tried everything—maybe even counseling (e.g., a facilitator or consultant), but the marriage between you and your Friends group is irretrievably broken. You might feel there is nothing else you can do except wait for them to end their volunteer activities as they move into a nursing home.

The truth is, there is something you can do, and, in fact, if your Friends group is dysfunctional and actually standing in the way of what could be a different, strong, robust, and engaging group, you actually have a responsibility to do everything you can to open the pathway for a new group to form. This isn't an easy or pleasant step to take, and you might get some negative feedback. You'll know when you're ready to take this step, and you won't be doing it alone.

First of all, if you have a governing board, you must discuss this issue with them (if you haven't already). Let them know what you've done to try to remedy the situation. It's likely they'll have some ideas as well and may be reluctant at first to take any drastic steps. Give them some time to get used to the idea of asking the Friends to disband. It's important that you do what you can to get your trustees on your page.

Governing boards have the authority and fiduciary responsibility to protect the library's assets. This includes the name of the library. Though your trustees do not have authority over the Friends (assuming they are a separate 501(c)(3) organization), they do have authority over who uses the library's name.

Once the decision has been made by the board to disassociate with the Friends, the board should send a "cease and desist" letter to the Friends' board for using the library's name. In addition, the board should write a letter to the editor thanking the Friends for past service and explaining in a clear, non-emotional way why the board is taking this action. If the library plans to work to develop a new Friends group, an invitation to new recruits asking new volunteers to contact the library director can be included in the letter to the editor. As mentioned before, there is likely to be some pushback, but if your reasons are solid, you need simply stand by them.

If you do not have a board or if your board is advisory only, you still have a path that you can take. In this case, you should meet with your direct supervisor—the city or county manager or the mayor. It'll be an easier course with a paid administrator, because he or she will be less worried about any political fallout such a move might have.

A mayor or other elected official to whom you report will most certainly be concerned about political fallout. If this is the case with you, you will want to have solid evidence that extends over a year at least documenting conversations you've had, money they've collected for the library but have not released, and money they've spent elsewhere. Be sure to let the mayor know that you are planning to start a new group if this is the case, and you might even sweeten the effort with him or her by stating a monetary goal you believe a new Friends group could bring within the next three years—being sure the goal well exceeds what the Friends have given over the past three years.

If you are unsuccessful getting your board or your boss to take action on disallowing the Friends to use the library's name in your fundraising, you could consider instead starting a foundation or working with the foundation to engage more on the grassroots level. You might also consider starting a new group with a different name, but that would undoubtedly cause even more confusion among community donors. In the end, if you aren't able to secure authorization to send out the "cease and desist" letter, consider working with them as best you can, or even not working with them at all and put this relationship at the very bottom of your worry list.

STRONG FRIENDS =
STRONG LIBRARY SUPPORT

Libraries across the country have been benefiting for years by wonderful Friends groups that want nothing more than to help make their library the very best it can be. They happily engage in fundraising activities, they promote and advocate for the library when needed, and they work hand in hand with the library administration in order to provide exactly what the library needs.

It seems true that the most high-functioning Friends groups have strong, visible support from the library. I believe that because Friends are so important, the library director should attend their meetings and functions. It will honor the Friends and show them that they are an important component for development, advocacy, community engagement, and library promotion.

No matter how hard you work, there may be times when—because leadership of the Friends turns over, or a former director neglected them, or for a myriad of personality problems—Friends become unfriendly. This can and does cause many headaches for the library director and can, in fact, cause poor publicity for the library when and if these dysfunctional relationships become public. In addition, these groups make it almost impossible to create a new high-functioning board when they hold onto their name as "Friends of the Library."

It's always best to take the time and trouble to mend poor relationships, but in the end, you might have to work to disband them. Understand that when this becomes the only option, it also becomes the best option. It is your responsibility to ensure that unfriendly groups don't remain Friends with you.

Ideas to Steal—Taking Your Friends from Good to Great

MY ORGANIZATION, UNITED FOR LIBRARIES: THE ASSOCIATION OF TRUSTEES, Advocates, Friends and Foundations, has collected many great ideas from both academic and public libraries over the years. This chapter will share the best of the best ideas in fundraising, events, programming, membership, and advocacy. Hopefully, these great ideas will help you work more closely with your Friends group to employ some of them and stimulate greater engagement with your community or campus, and even help you grow your group!

MEMBERSHIP

CREDIT UNION INCENTIVE

Members of the Friends of the Stoneham Public Library (Massachusetts) are eligible to join the Stoneham Municipal Employees Federal Credit Union. Applications to join both the credit union and the Friends of the Library are made available at the circulation desk.

AQUATIC AND FITNESS INCENTIVE

The Friends of the Allen Public Library (Texas) held a membership drive for "60 New Friends in 60 Summer Days." Those who joined during a two-month period in the summer received two free one-day passes to the Don Rodenbaugh Natatorium, a local aquatic and fitness center. Also in Allen, those who join the Friends of the Allen Public Library for $10 or more receive ten overdue fine waivers at the library—a "Get Out of Jail Free" card!

AN EVENING WITH FRIENDS

The Friends of the Sherratt Library at Southern Utah University (SUU) held an inaugural gala with the theme "An Evening with Friends." More than 150 guests attended the gala and enjoyed music, food, and camaraderie. Special guests included photographers Homer S. Jones and Max R. Bonzo, who both spent many years in Cedar City and donated their collections of photographs and negatives to the SUU Library Archives. Photography exhibits were displayed throughout the library for guests to enjoy as they moved from floor to floor. Refreshments were served on every floor, with the main course on the second floor in the Huntsman Reading Room. SUU faculty authors exhibited their books on the third floor. Some also read from their publications and showed videos they produced. The SUU jazz ensemble, string ensemble, and piano music created an atmosphere of warmth and welcome. More than 70 people joined the Friends of a Sherratt Library as a result of the gala.

HANDMADE BOOKS

The Friends of Henderson Libraries at Georgia Southern University (Statesboro) commissioned Georgia Southern senior Tami Henry to create handmade books for lifetime members of the Friends. Using handmade papers, she hand-bound a small, unique creation that holds blank pages for writing or drawing. Henry utilized Coptic stitching and additional decorative stitches with wax thread for the binding. Each book contained unlined cotton pulp paper sewn together and was covered with handmade papers. Henry included a colophon within each work that provided details on the materials, the date of the book, and her signature.

GRAND PRIZE RAFFLE

For National Library Week, the Orange County Library System (Orlando, Florida) invited customers to join the Friends of the Orange County Library. Those who joined or upgraded their membership before Friday were eligible to win grand prizes, including two AirTran Airways tickets, a Ritz-Carlton Orlando Grande Lakes getaway, a Grand Bohemian Hotel Orlando getaway, and a $50 gift card to Chick-fil-A.

APPRECIATION DINNER

The Friends of the Kershaw County Library (Camden, South Carolina) held an appreciation dinner for members who joined at the $300-plus level. Marianne Gingher, an award-winning author and professor of creative writing at the University of North Carolina at Chapel Hill, spoke at the dinner, which was held at the Robert Mills Courthouse in Camden. Friends who joined at the $100-plus level were invited on a guided woodland walk along Native American and Civil War trails in the area.

DOLLAR MATCH CHALLENGE

A match challenge from longtime University of North Carolina Libraries (Chapel Hill) supporter Howard Holsenbeck added $100 to the first 100 new Friends memberships of at least $100 each. Gifts were required to be made by the end of the year. "Giving to the Library is one of the best investments I've ever made," said Holsenbeck, a member of the University of North Carolina-Chapel Hill class of 1963. "I'd like to encourage others to join me." Holsenbeck's support for the library reaches back to the year of his graduation, when he sent $50 to what he called "the most important part of the university." Since then, he has made a gift every single year, often several a year, to support the collections of the university library. A previous Holsenbeck challenge doubled ten gifts of $1,000 from new donors to the library. "Howard Holsenbeck epitomizes the generosity of our Friends of the Library," said University Librarian Sarah Michalak. "He wants to share the sense of purpose and commitment with others by encouraging them to give to the library, too."

BRANCH MEMBERSHIP ADD-ON

Anyone who joins the Friends of Hennepin County Library (Minneapolis, Minnesota) receives membership to the Friends group of the local branch library of their choice. The membership then supports both system-wide book purchases and programs at the member's local library.

GIFT BAG RAFFLE

Those who renewed their membership in the Friends of Belleville Library (Kansas) were entered to win a "Kansas Gift Bag" full of goodies donated by the Friends board members. The basket was given to one lucky Friends member at the Friends annual meeting.

LOCAL BUSINESS DISCOUNTS

The Friends of the L.E. Phillips Memorial Public Library (Eau Claire, Wisconsin) teamed with local businesses to offer special discounts to Friends members. Participating merchants were Obsession Chocolates (10 percent off any purchase), Crossroad Books (15 percent off any purchase), The Coffee Grounds (10 percent off espresso beverages or bulk coffee), Tangled Up in Hue (10 percent off any purchase), and Chippewa Valley Theatre Guild ($2 off adult/senior tickets and $1 off youth tickets). In addition, Friends members save $1 off any purchase of $10 or more on Friday Friends of the Library book sales.

The Friends of the Del Webb Library (Indian Land, South Carolina) partner with local businesses to encourage membership in their organization while also promoting patronage at those businesses. More than 20 local businesses offer discounts on their products and services to persons who present their Friends membership card.

PET MEMBERSHIP

The Friends of the Covington Library (Washington) offers an opportunity for pets to support the library through honorary Friends membership. When a former staff member said she was going to have her cats join the Friends, it was discussed at a Friends meeting; Friends decided that pets would pay the adult membership fee but would not have voting rights, be

> ## TOP TEN REASONS TO BE A FRIEND
>
> The Friends of the Arapahoe Library District (Englewood, Colorado) printed "The Top Ten Reasons to be a Friends of the Library" in its library newsletter. The reasons were:
>
> 10. You are welcomed to the exclusive Preview Sale at the annual Used Book Sale.
> 9. You receive a 20-percent off coupon for use in one of our used book stores.
> 8. You are invited to the annual Friends Holiday Party—always a memorable affair!
> 7. You help kids learn to read by supporting summer reading and other literacy programs.
> 6. You assist in the advancement of new technology initiatives for the library and its community.
> 5. You meet and mix with other Friends.
> 4. You provide tax-deductible contributions.
> 3. You serve as an ambassador for the library.
> 2. You help build a literate, informed, and fulfilled community.
> 1. You love the library.

able to participate in programs, or come to meetings. Pets are honorary members. Since then, cats, dogs, and birds have all been members of the Friends of the Covington Library.

OPEN HOUSE

The Friends of the Lucy Robbins Welles Library (Newington, Connecticut) held an open house to introduce Friends members (and potential Friends members) to the volunteer opportunities available to them. Printed information on the book sale committee, the membership committee, the hospitality committee, and various other committees was distributed, and committee representatives were available to answer questions. Members filled out interest forms, and as a result of the open house, the Friends gained several new volunteers.

MEMBERSHIP PACKAGE

At an annual meeting of the Friends of the Riverside Library (California), Membership Chair Pamela Moore presented plans for a major membership drive in the next year. In an effort to expand membership to 500, the board developed a package of membership benefits for new members, including a book bag, coupons for DVD rentals, a coupon for up to $5 at book sales, and a monthly emailed update about library activities. Although in the past, memberships were renewed in the month in which the member first joined, it was decided they would all now be due in April, the month of the annual meeting. During the first year of changing membership dates, dues were prorated to provide for a partial year membership, putting everyone due for a full year in April the following year.

ANGEL TREE

The Friends of the Ida Long Goodman Memorial Library (St. John, Kansas) hosted an "Angel Tree" during the holiday season. The tree was decorated with red (adult) and white (children) book cutouts with the title, author, and cost of a book from the library's wish list. An angel pin was on the book card for the patron to keep. When a patron purchased a book for the library, the Friends gave the purchaser a membership to the Friends.

MONTHLY DONATIONS

The Newport Beach Public Library Foundation (California) offers monthly donations as one of its membership/giving options. "It's as inexpensive as a cup of coffee. Or a magazine. Or an ice cream. What is it? The new and ultra-easy monthly donation option—a small amount that when multiplied by many donors makes an enormous difference in the services we're able to offer." Monthly donation options start at $5 and go up to $35 and provide benefits including discounts to local businesses.

FRIEND OF THE LIBRARY MEMBERSHIP CARD

Those who join the Friends of the Santa Clarita Library (California) receive an exclusive "Friend of the Library" library card. Members can then use the card for special entry to book sales and events. The thank-you letter sent by the Friends to new members lets them know that they just need to bring in the letter/email and then they can get the exclusive library card for Friends members.

MEMBERSHIP INCENTIVES

The Friends of Westlake Porter Public Library (Ohio) have a nice list of incentives to join the Friends, including:

- 5 percent discount at Dean's Greenhouse.
- A coupon for a scoop of delicious ice cream from a popular local vendor.
- A "Used Book Buck" worth $1 toward a purchase in the Friends' Book Nook.
- 10 percent discount at Portables Gift Shop in the library.
- Admission to Preview Night for the Friends' Book Sale.

COUPON BOOKLETS

Those who become members of the Friends of the Guntersville Public Library (Alabama) are entered into a drawing for coupon booklets worth cash for purchases at the library. Members joining at any level receive one chance to win. Members joining at the patron, benefactor, sponsor, or underwriter levels receive a second chance to win.

SPECIAL BOOKS BUYING OPPORTUNITY

The Friends of the Kirkwood Public Library (Kansas) have a special benefit for their members. The book sale committee selects special books and makes them available at a special price—usually half or less than half the price of their normal asking price—for one month to members only. They stipulate that a "special book" is old, rare, a first edition, out-of-print, or in some way "special." A sample listing is:

> "Carrington, Frances C. Army Life on the Plains: My Army Life and the Fort Phil Kearney Massacre. With an Account of the Celebration of 'Wyoming Opened.' J.B. Lippincott. 1910. Dark green hardback. Spine is scuffed, soiled, and loosened. Interior good, black print with foldout map and historical photos and illustrations. The author's personal narrative of army life as a young officer's wife in 1866. $40."

CHAMBER OF COMMERCE PARTNERSHIP

The Friends of the Mount Prospect Public Library (Illinois) handed out free books and membership applications at a Chamber of Commerce's Midsummer Downtown Block Party. As a result, they were able to recruit a number of new volunteers from families that visited their booth.

GIFT OF MEMBERSHIP

The Friends of the L.E. Phillips Memorial Library (Eau Claire, Wisconsin) encourage their members to buy a membership in their group for friends and family at the holidays. It's a great idea for those who have everything, and perhaps recipients will renew their memberships in the year ahead!

SPECIAL INVITATIONS

As part of membership recruitment efforts, library patrons and Friends were invited to look for special mailings and Friends ambassadors at select library branches. When you become a Friend of the St. Louis Public Library (Missouri), you receive the Foundation's newsletter, invitations and reserved seating for author events, invitations to Friends events, and the knowledge that you helped provide the opportunity for millions in the St. Louis region to access a world of information.

LUNCH WITH AN AUTHOR RAFFLE

The Friends of the Phoenix Public Library (Arizona) provide an incentive for current members to renew by entering them into a drawing to win lunch with a local bestselling author, along with three of the winner's friends (as long as they, too, are also members). The contest is open to existing members only. This is a great way to engage local authors and encourage members to renew.

OPEN HOUSE

The Friends of the Loveland Public Library Foundation (Colorado) hosted an open house for all of the group's "checkbook" members during the summer to meet members of the board and committee chairs, and to learn about their many fun activities and opportunities. Popcorn and ice cream were served, and a quiz about library history livened up the afternoon.

MEMBERSHIP CATEGORIES

The Friends of the Library and Archives (FOLA) at Kettering University (Flint, Michigan) promotes membership in its quarterly newsletter by letting readers know that FOLA membership is open to anyone interested in supporting the Kettering University Library and Archives. Member categories include student, senior citizen, individual, or family, and each may be taken out for one, two, or three years, with discounts for a two- or three-year membership. All memberships are tax-deductible donations to Kettering University. Members receive a quarterly newsletter, as well as advance notice on programs and events, and are able to check out library materials. Most importantly, members help advance the Kettering Library and Archives as crucial centers of learning at the university.

FRIENDS' COOKBOOK

The Friends of Kodak Library (Tennessee) awarded complimentary memberships to Citizens National Bank's Kodak Branch, Food City of Kodak, and Kodak Trade Center, in appreciation of the wonderful job they have done selling the Friends' *A Second Helping of the Kodak Historical Cookbook*. In one fiscal year, the three businesses sold more than $1,000 worth of cookbooks.

RECESSION SPECIAL

The Friends of the Burbank Public Library (California) offered a "Recession Special" in 2009 for those whose membership expired over the summer. Members could renew through Dec. 31, 2009, and their membership was in good standing through Dec. 31, 2010, which offered up to six months of free membership. Dues remained at the same low prices—$15 (Friend) to $500 (Lifetime Friend).

FUNDRAISING

WE LOVE NC BBQ @ THE LIBRARY

The Friends of Library at the University of North Carolina at Pembroke (UNCP—Pembroke) hosted "We Love NC BBQ @ the Library" in the Mary Livermore Library. The event featured speaker John Shelton Reed, coauthor of *Holy Smoke: The Big Book of North Carolina Barbecue*. Local barbecue expert Bobby Jacobs cooked a pig on the library's patio, and a variety of food stations offered Southern side dishes. In addition to the dinner, there was a silent auction and a live auction for items including a five-day Bahamas cruise, a framed photo of Elizabeth Taylor, an autographed script from the TV show *M*A*S*H,* and a stay at the Grove Park Resort and Spa in Asheville, North Carolina. Funds raised at the event supported Friends of the Library initiatives such as continuing support for UNCP scholarships, funding a leasing program for popular reading materials and audiobooks, and author appearances and reading programs.

DINNER PARTNERSHIP

Friends of the Union County Library (Blairsville, Georgia) and Brother's Restaurant in Murphy, North Carolina, teamed up for a Community Night fundraiser. The Friends received 15 percent of dinner sales that evening. Proceeds were used to purchase furnishings and fixtures for the library expansion and renovation.

COMMUNITY ARTS EVENT

The Arapahoe Library District Friends Foundation (Englewood, Colorado) held "The Tile Project," a community art event and fundraiser for children and adults. On one day a week for three weeks, hundreds of six-by-six inch tiles were available for $25 each. Participants hand-painted the tiles, and then they were kiln-fired by Color Me Mine and installed as a permanent display outside the concierge lobby at the new Streets at South Glenn retail center.

DIAMOND JACKPOT

The Friends of the Georgetown Library (South Carolina) sponsored a catered, ticketed event titled "Diamonds in the Rough." Guests who purchased $25 tickets enjoyed catered cuisine by Puttin' on the Ritz, as well as live entertainment. With each glass of champagne purchased, guests received a "diamond." The "diamonds" were cubic zirconia, with the exception of one genuine half-carat diamond. Champagne drinkers found out who the lucky winner was by taking their "gem" to Sonny Burgoon, a certified gemologist from the Diamond Collection. Burgoon also offered free verbal jewelry appraisals and written appraisals for a small charge during the event.

GROCERY PURCHASE DONATIONS

On a special shopping day, 5 percent of all purchases made at the Whole Foods Market at the Streets at South Glenn retail center were donated to the Arapahoe Library District Friends Foundation (Englewood, Colorado). The library encouraged supporters to "stock up on groceries, eat some sushi, visit the coffee bar, enjoy European-style baked goods, buy organic, and feel good that your purchases will make a difference to the Arapahoe Library District."

TOTE BAGS AND T-SHIRTS

The Library Foundation of Hennepin County (Minneapolis, Minnesota) sells tote bags and T-shirts with the Hennepin County Library logo. The tote bag is available in two designs, one with the text "Got books?" and another with the quote "Libraries will get you through times of no money better than money will get you through times of no libraries." Both cost $8.60. The T-shirt features "Got books?" on the front and the Hennepin County Library logo on the back, and is available in both women's and men's sizes. The cost is $15.

KIDS COUNT: CAN THEY COUNT ON YOU?

The Riverside Public Library Foundation (California) began a campaign to help replace children's classics in the library, an expenditure that takes one-quarter of the children's materials budget. The campaign slogan is "Kids Count: Can They Count on You?" Banners and posters featuring the campaign slogan were displayed in all branch libraries.

DON'T COME TO TEA

The Friends of the Bergenfield Library (New Jersey) "hosted" a "Don't Come to a Tea Party" fundraiser. The "invite" read, "What we *won't* be serving: scones, crumpets, muffins, tea breads, ladyfingers, cookies, cakes, or mints." The non-event asked participants to "Stay home and enjoy a cup of tea on us. But remember to send us $5 per non-guest in the enclosed envelope." This clever non-event saved time and money while still raising funds for the library.

FRIENDS & FLAGS RECEPTION

The Friends of Libraries & Archives of Texas and the Atascocito Historical Society co-hosted a "Friends & Flags" reception at the Sam Houston Regional Library and Research Center (Liberty, Texas). Close to 100 guests enjoyed the evening, which included a display of two Texas treasures from the Lorenzo de Zavala State Archives and Library Building.

DRAMA & FRIENDS PARTNERSHIP

The Friends of the Hartington Public Library (Nebraska) teamed up with a local acting group for a first-time joint fundraiser—and murder was on the menu. The murder mystery dinner theater combined local talent from the Cedar County Theater Group, along with a few folks from the Friends group. Over-the-top character performances shined throughout the sold-out evening, as a four-course meal for 100 was served by the Friends between acts. This performance event, held at a local country club, started with a cash bar social hour at 6 P.M., and a lasagna meal began at 6:45 P.M. The overwhelming response and success of this event led to speculation of future performances with double capacity for seating.

GADGET REPAIR

The Speedway Public Library (Indiana) offered a "DVD, CD & Game Disc Repair Day." DVDs, CDs, and video game discs were repaired via machine at the cost of three discs for $1. Drop-off was available from 9 A.M.–3 P.M. and pick-up was 4–5 P.M. Proceeds benefited the Friends of the Speedway Public Library for future library programs.

BOWL-A-THON

The Friends of the Library of Rio Rancho (New Mexico) sponsored a Bowl-A-Thon at Tenpins & More. Team sponsorship cost $50, which covered bowling, shoe rentals, and T-shirts for five bowlers. Prizes included books, Chick-fil-A coupons, coupons for free massages and haircuts, and WWE tickets. In 2009, the Bowl-A-Thon raised enough funds to offset the city's 2009 cuts to library programs.

STRING QUARTET

The Friends of the Arcata Library (California) hosted the Giovanni String Quartet for a benefit concert. The quartet played to a standing-room-only crowd of 150, and earned $1,200 for the Friends. The concert took place inside the Arcata Library after hours. A welcome reception followed, with food and drink donated by local eateries, including Safeway and Starbucks.

BOOK APPRAISAL FAIR

The Friends of the Northern Illinois University Libraries (DeKalb) hosted a book appraisal fair in the rare books and special collections department. Appraisals were provided by Thomas Joyce of Thomas J. Joyce & Co., the Chicago Rare Book Center, and William Butts of Main Street Fine Books in Galena, Illinois. Butts, who has appeared on PBS's *History Detectives*, has extensive experience with appraising ephemera and autographs. Individual appraisals cost $10 per title. Members of the Friends received their first three appraisals for free, and subsequent appraisals at the discounted rate of $5 each. Friends membership applications were accepted on site.

LIBRARY MINIATURES FOR SALE

The Friends of the Marshall Public Library (Illinois) purchased wooden miniatures of the library building to sell. The miniatures are a drawing of the library on a wooden block, complete with a brief history of the library on the back. The cost is $20, payable to the Friends. Other Marshall miniatures (including replicas of the high school, First United Methodist Church, Clark County Court House, and more) are available through the Terre Haute Children's Museum.

MOTHER'S DAY GARDEN TOUR

The Friends of Trinidad Library (California) hosted a Mother's Day Garden Tour. Tickets cost $5 and were available at several garden stores and Blake's Books. The ticket included several gardens, a plant sale, and refreshments on the patio of Trinidad Museum. In December, the Trinidad Lights Holiday Home Tour raised $1,000 for the Friends.

FAMILY NIGHT AT THE LIBRARY

The Friends of the Loveland Public Library Foundation (Colorado) hosted "A Night at the Library," offering many activities for children, including a pizza dinner, dessert, a magic act, photo sessions with *Star Wars* characters, cooking lessons, and dancing lessons. Tickets were $20, $18 in advance, to benefit the library's capital campaign.

ANTIQUE APPRAISAL NIGHT

The Ponte Vedra Beach Friends of the Library (Florida) presented an Antique Appraisal Showcase at the library. In the spirit of the popular television show *Antiques Roadshow*, the Friends invited the public to find out whether their antiques were indeed treasures. Ten local appraisers gave attendees appraisals on up to two items. A donation of $5 per item to the Friends was suggested. Appraisers were on hand for books, coins, dolls, fine art, fine jewelry, military items, and general antiques.

LIBRARY LIBATIONS WINETASTING

The Friends of the Kirkwood Public Library (Missouri) held Library Libations, a wine-tasting fundraiser, at Grapevine Wines. Fifty-nine people attended, enjoyed hors d'oeuvres, and learned about wines. The Friends raised more than $1,900 from the event, which came from ticket sales, raffle tickets sold, and 10 percent of sales made by Grapevine Wines.

LITERARY VOICES BENEFIT

The Friends of the Libraries of the University of Washington (Seattle) holds an annual "Literary Voices" benefit at the University of Washington Club. One year the keynote speaker was Timothy Egan, who worked for 18 years as opinion columnist for the *New York Times*, as its Pacific Northwest correspondent, and as a national enterprise reporter. Attendees were invited to dine at Literary Roundtables with featured authors, including Paul Bannick, Heather McHugh, Knute Berger, and David B. Williams. Tickets cost $100.

BOOKPLATES FOR STUDENTS

Every year, Georgetown Law parents have the chance to honor their graduating seniors by making a $100 donation to the Georgetown Law

Library (Washington, D.C.). This recognition is memorialized in a commemorative bookplate inserted into one of the library's new books. The bookplates can also be used for other recognition opportunities.

SLEUTH SOIREE

The Friends of the Cary Memorial Library, Inc. (Lexington, Massachusetts) held a "Sleuth Soiree," a successful fundraiser featuring mystery writers Katherine Hall Page, Jane Langston, William Tapply, Vicki Stiefel, Valerie Wolzien, Andrew McAleer, Linda Barnes, William Martin, and Hank Phillippi Ryan. The authors spoke, signed copies of their books, and mingled with guests in a Halloween party setting. Ticket proceeds ($75 per person) and a silent auction brought in $6,000 for the library.

UNBELIEVABLE CHOCOLATE RAFFLE

The Mount Prospect Public Library Foundation (Illinois) enjoys sweet success at the group's annual "Unbelievable Chocolate Raffle," held in February. One year, the event featured 12 specialty-themed baskets, each designed for a specific type of chocolate lover. The baskets were on display in the lobby of the library so visitors could see the items firsthand and purchase raffle tickets from a Foundation volunteer. Tickets cost $1 each or six tickets for $5. Most of the raffle items were donated by area retailers and board members. Names and contents of the baskets ranged from "Oscar Worthy Chocolate," which featured gourmet chocolates and movie passes donated by a local movie theater, to "Will Work for Chocolate," which included a generous assortment of hearty chocolate treats along with professional hand tools donated by the Robert Bosch Tool Corporation. The event concluded with a grand drawing held on Valentine's Day at the library. The event raised $4,500 for the Foundation, which provides additional funding for special events and other services at the library.

TOWN SPELLING BEE

The Friends of the Dover Library (Massachusetts) holds an annual "Dover Town Spelling Bee." The Bee is broadcast live on Dover Cable Television. Dover's finest spellers—in teams of three—are invited to join the competition for the title and grand prize of "Enormous Bragging Rights." The entry fee per person is $300, and each team can purchase a "mulligan" to help them for $100.

CRAFTS FOR CHRISTMAS

When the Friends of the Babcock Library (Ashford, Connecticut) came across an old maroon-colored stage curtain that had been dumped in a corner and was soon to be discarded, the group had the idea to transform it into salable items. Friends members washed the curtain, then made from it Christmas tree skirts, purses, stuffed animals, table runners, and ornaments. The group sold the items at various events held at the library and raised more than $5,000. This project won the Focused Project Award for municipalities of less than 15,000 residents from the Friends of Connecticut Libraries.

WINE TASTING AND AUCTION

The Friends of the Tellico Village Library (Loudon, Tennessee) hosts an annual Wine Tasting. The event was expanded to include a silent auction. In addition, sponsor United Community Bank of Tellico Village hosted a Tailgate Party for Tellico Village residents from 10 A.M. to 2 P.M. as a prelude to the event. Merchandise designed and created by a local resident was sold at the event, with all proceeds going to the Tellico Village Library Building Fund. Tickets to the wine tasting and silent auction event cost $35, $30 for Friends members.

TEXTILE FUNDRAISER

The Friends of the Thomas Crane Public Library (Quincy, Massachusetts) held a textile fundraiser to raise money for library programs. The Friends accepted unwanted clothing, shoes, linens, curtains, fabrics, and small toys at trailers located at five local schools. The Friends earned $50 for every ton donated, and an additional $500 for every ten tons collected. The fundraiser was managed by Quincy's department of public works on behalf of the Friends.

FRANKLY, WE LOVE OUR LIBRARY BBQ

The Edgartown Library Foundation (Massachusetts) hosts an annual barbecue event, "Frankly, We Love Our Library," at Katama Airfield on Labor Day. Approximately 450 people attend the event, enjoying frankfurters and ice cream sundaes. Activities include face painting, a climbing wall, a bounce house, field races, and a chance to check out a fire truck courtesy of the Edgartown Fire Department. The Martha's Vineyard Model Flying Club displays scale model aircraft and gives guests an opportunity to make their own gliders and test their wings with a flight simulator.

THE LITERARY VINE

More than 250 people attended "The Literary Vine," a fundraiser hosted by the Friends of Richland County Public Library (Columbia, South Carolina). The first-time event raised more than $10,000 and featured more than 30 varieties of wine and an array of foods. The Literary Vine was sponsored by Blue Cross Blue Shield of South Carolina, Southern Wine and Spirits, and Bonefish Grill. Additional sponsors included Carrabba's Italian Grill, Coastal States Bank, Colonial Life, Control Management, Inc., Dianne's on Devine, Immaculate Consumption, Gervais and Vine, Tiffany's Bakery, Turner Padget Graham & Laney, P.A., MarketSearch, and Wachovia.

LIVE AUCTION

The Friends of the Waynesboro-Wayne County Library (Waynesboro, Mississippi) raised $2,325 from the sale of more than 100 items sold at a live auction, featuring items contributed by individuals and local businesses. After light refreshments were served, auctioneer Charles Seeger and assistant Kathy Walker entertained the crowd and sold items to the highest bidder, which resulted in a very successful evening for the Friends. The Friends donated the proceeds from the auction to help offset recent budget cutbacks.

BLING FOR BOOKS

The Friends of the Trinidad (California) Library hosted "Bling for Books," a silent auction of more than 300 necklaces, bracelets, rings, pins, and jewelry boxes given by donors. Raffle tickets were sold, and the winner received a large stained-glass window.

FALL CLASSIC RAFFLE

The Mount Prospect Public Library (MPPL—Illinois) Foundation holds an annual Fall Classic Raffle. One raffle featured 12 autumn-themed baskets displayed in the lobby of the library and raised more than $4,100 for the MPPL Foundation. Items ranged from gift certificates to area restaurants and theaters, to fall fashion and seasonal culinary treats. Volunteers sold tickets for $1 each or six for $5. The money raised is used by the MPPL Foundation to sponsor special events and programs that otherwise would not be available through public funding.

HANDMADE BOOK BAGS

The Collingswood Friends of the Library (New Jersey), along with the Collingswood Public Library, put out a call to the creative people in its community who like to sew, either by machine or by hand. Crafty folks were asked to make one-of-a-kind fabric book bags—which also happen to be good for shopping, toting, and general all-around use—out of donated fabric. The Friends then sold the finished bags for $10 each at the library, helping to fund programming, acquisitions, technology upgrades, and physical improvements to the library itself. The bag had a simple pattern and didn't take long to sew, and participants made great-looking bags out of reclaimed pants, skirts, and other garments, as well as other scraps of unwanted fabric. Volunteers precut the fabric to the pattern, and bundled it with instructions. These bundles were available for pickup at the library, along with assorted scrap fabric, art supplies, and findings that crafters could use to make these bags into fabulously unique book totes. The project was an ongoing fundraiser, but to get things started, the Collingswood Friends of the Library hosted an all-ages book bag sewing workshop. Participants were charged a $5 fee, which covered all materials, as well as use of a sewing machine. Volunteers provided help for those who needed it. The donations went to the Friends, and the bags went to the ongoing book tote sale.

BOOK IT! 5K WALK/RUN

In addition to raising money for the new Children's Outdoor Reading Garden and the opening collection of the newly reconstructed Roseville Library (Minnesota), the Friends of the Ramsey County Libraries sponsored a "Book It!" 5K Walk/Run. This race increased the library's visibility with younger members of the community. The event also helped transform the image of Friends from a group of retirees to a more dynamic and age-diverse organization. More than 360 people ranging in age from

2 to 75 and 50 volunteers participated in the event, which netted more than $3,800. The short-term results and long-term impact greatly exceeded expectations. The "Book It!" 5K Walk/Run became an annual Friends' fundraiser. This project won the Minnesota Association of Library Friends' Evy Nordley Best Project by Friends Award.

GOLD RUSH BOOK FAIR

The Friends of the Libraries of Nevada County (Grass Valley, California) held a "Gold Rush Book Fair" at the Nevada County Fairgrounds. More than 30 dealers were featured at the fair, offering out-of-print, rare, and collectible books and ephemera in all price ranges.

FARM TO TABLE DINNER

The Friends of Henderson Library at Georgia Southern University (Statesboro) hosts an annual "Farm to Table Dinner" each summer. Advance tickets cost $65 ($75 at the event). At one dinner, Chef Campbell of Christopher's Restaurant designed a five-course menu, featuring local produce and farm products paired with wine. The event is a fundraiser for the Henderson Library, as well as a showcase for the Statesboro Farmers Market and the produce grown in Bulloch County. All proceeds benefit the Henderson Library to enable it to keep pace with Georgia Southern's growth and future research needs. The first "Farm to Table Dinner" raised more than $1,600.

BRICKS FOR SALE

Friends of the Spring Hill College Library (Mobile, Alabama) sold bricks from the old Campus Center and Cloister at the Burke Library circulation desk. Only a few were set aside for sale, as the majority were recycled for use in the "green" building of the new Campus Center. A unique gift for alumni or current members of the college community, the bricks sold for $100 each, and all proceeds benefited the Friends. In addition, purchase of a brick included a one-year membership to the Friends.

PRE-OSCAR EVENT

The Newport Beach Public Library Foundation (California) held a special pre-Oscar event, "The Road to the Oscars," with Robert Kline. Kline, a producer, presented a two-hour program devoted to the Academy Awards, including Oscar history, the nominations, and film clips from the major contenders. A Q&A followed. The event was held at the Lido Theatre. Tickets cost $25, and a portion of the proceeds benefited the Newport Beach Public Library Foundation.

BASKETBALL TICKET SALES

San Antonio Public Library (Texas) held "San Antonio Public Library Night with the Spurs." A portion of the ticket sales from the San Antonio Spurs basketball game (versus the Dallas Mavericks) benefited the library. Those who purchased tickets were asked to use the special promotion code "library."

WINE AT THE YACHT CLUB

The Friends of the Tellico Village Library (Loudon, Tennessee) held its second annual wine tasting at the Yacht Club. Approximately 330 people attended the event, which was expanded to include a silent auction. The event raised $10,000 for the building fund of the new Tellico Village Public Library.

DINNER WITH THE FRIENDS

The Friends of the Library at the University of Massachusetts-Amherst hosts an annual "Dinner with Friends" at the W.E.B. Du Bois Library. One year the celebration began with a champagne and hors d'oeuvre reception and live music by UMass-Amherst student musicians. The evening continued with a gourmet dinner, talks by guest speakers Gretchen Holbrook Gerzina and Roy Blount Jr., and a book signing. Tickets cost $140 per person, or $250 for two (of which $95 was tax deductible, $160 for two). Proceeds benefited the W.E.B. Du Bois Center.

BOOKS 'N BOIL CELEBRATION

The Friends of the Florence County Library (South Carolina) held a "Books 'n' Boil" celebration, which featured chefs and cookbook authors Matt and Ted Lee. The Lee brothers judged a chef competition from each of the branch libraries. The celebration also featured a silent auction, champagne reception, entertainment by the Blue Iguanas, as well as a Southern staple—boiled peanuts.

QUIZ NIGHT AT THE LIBRARY

Friends of Coquitlam Public Library (B.C., Canada) hosted a Quiz Night. Participants could sign up in teams of eight, or sign up individually and be placed with a team. Topics included geography, history, current events, and literature. Tickets cost $25 and included coffee, dessert, and a chance to win prizes. Proceeds supported literacy projects for children and adults, including the library's book bus.

LIBRARY GALA

The Friends of the Sherratt Library (Cedar City, Utah) holds an annual library gala in the fall. As the group's main fundraising event, the gala showcases the library, and one year the gala featured the 1623 First Folio of Shakespeare's plays, on loan from the Folger Library in Washington, D.C. Utah Shakespeare Festival (USF) Founder Fred Adams was on hand to give insight into the history and importance of the Folio. Adjunct history professor and author Ryan Paul discussed researching the USF archives that were recently given to the library and writing *Celebrate 50 Years: Utah Shakespeare Festival*. The photo exhibit *We Are Such Stuff as Dreams are Made On*, celebrating the 50 years of the Utah Shakespeare Festival, was on display. Dean Shauna Mendini and Southern Utah University (SUU) students of the College of Performing and Visual Arts gave a presentation about their recent trip to China, where they presented *The Dream of Helen*, the dance drama inspired by the life and achievements of Cedar City native Helen Foster Snow. In addition, a string quartet and jazz ensemble from the SUU Music Department provided music throughout the evening. The cost was $35, which included membership in the Friends of the Library at the patron level.

ASSISTED LIVING COOKOUT FOR BOOKS

Peninsula Friends of the Library (Rancho Palos Verdes, California) held a "Cookout for Books" at Belmont Village Assisted Living. For a tax-deductible donation of $15 ($5 children), attendees enjoyed burgers, chicken, and other grilled favorites.

10 FOR TEN

Friends of the Memphis Libraries (Tennessee) responded generously to a "10 for Ten" campaign launched by the Memphis Library Foundation to honor and commemorate the 10th anniversary of the Benjamin L. Hooks (Main) Library. Contributing to the year-long goal of raising $500,000, the Friends donated funds to cover the cost and installation of software supporting the library's digital projects, such as local history and Memphis music. During a ceremony attended by more than 500 people, the Friends presented a check for $24,000 to the Foundation. Honorary chairs for the event were Leigh Anne and Sean Touhy, who were the subjects of the movie *The Blind Side*. Mayor A.C. Wharton, Congressman Steve Cohen, and University of Memphis basketball coach Josh Pastner were also on hand to show their support for the library system.

MINI GOLF FOR THE LIBRARY

The Friends of the Westlake Porter Public Library (Ohio) rents out a nine-hole mini golf course that was built for the Friends by Eagle Scout James Augustryn. The rental cost is $100 for 48 hours, and includes nine holes of mini golf, putters, balls, and hole decorations.

GOODSEARCH BROWSER REVENUE SHARE

The Friends of the L.E. Phillips Memorial Public Library (Eau Claire, Wisconsin) has been designated as a GoodSearch.com recipient. Instead of using a regular web browser, those wishing to support the Friends can log on to www.goodsearch.com and designate their donation for their Friends. The average donation is about 1 cent per search query, and the results are powered by Yahoo! The website also includes GoodShop.com, which provides an online shop featuring more than 2,000 stores. Each purchase made via GoodShop results in a donation to the user's preferred charity, averaging about 3 percent of the sale.

DIGITAL GAME DEVELOPMENT SUMMER CAMP

The Mishawaka-Penn-Harris Public Library (Mishawaka, Indiana) held a Digital Game Development Summer Camp one summer at the Harris Branch Library. Teens ages 12–17 learned how to create a computer game before it goes to the coding and artwork stages. Teens were grouped into design teams to create their own games. The cost of the program was $60, to benefit the Friends of the Mishawaka-Penn-Harris Public Library.

RECURRING DONATION PROGRAM

The Newport Beach Public Library Foundation (California) has introduced a recurring donation program. On the Foundation's donation page, donors can choose the "recurring donation" option, and their credit card is charged monthly in the denomination they choose. If at any time they want to change the amount or frequency, or want to opt out, they can do so easily by accessing their personal library Foundation account. They are given usernames and passwords to access their accounts when they set up their recurring donation. The first 30 people to sign up for a recurring donation received a signed book by an author who has recently visited the library. Those able to give $25 per month will receive a pair of tickets for the Foundation's fall lecture series (valued at $100).

BOWLING FOR LIBRARY DOLLARS

The Friends of the Library of Rio Rancho, Inc. (New Mexico), hosts an annual Bowl-A-Thon. One year more than $1,000 was raised, which was used for children's programs at the library. More than 20 door prizes were donated and given, in addition to prizes for highest individual score, highest team score, and most pledges collected. Each bowler received three games, shoe rental, and a t-shirt.

A VOTE FOR MURDER

Friends of Handley Regional Library (Virginia) hosted "A Vote for Murder," an event that raised $5,700. More than 20 merchants and restaurants supplied food for the event.

COSTUME JEWELRY SALE

The Friends of Mountville (Pennsylvania) Branch Library held a very successful used costume jewelry sale, an idea they borrowed from the Oro Valley (Arizona) Friends. Each of these Friends groups has a sister in common that Skyped across the country about the jewelry idea. The Friends of Mountville Branch Library solicited donations of used costume jewelry from the public and were showered with beautiful (mostly!) used jewelry. The jewelry was then priced individually, with a knowledgeable Friend who makes jewelry overseeing their pricing. The jewelry was very reasonably priced and displayed in interesting ways for the enthusiastic shoppers. Not only did the sale raise much-needed funds of $2,100, the Friends and their numerous shoppers had a great time.

HOLIDAY E-CARDS

The New York Public Library (New York) offered holiday e-cards for those donating a minimum of $5 to the library. There were eight different cards to choose from, each featuring an image from the library's Digital Gallery. The e-card message (which could be edited) read "I have made a gift in your name to The New York Public Library. This gift will help ensure that all New Yorkers continue to have free access to crucial resources in the coming year. Best wishes for a joyous holiday season!"

MEET THE AUTHOR BLACK-TIE DINNER

The Friends of the Tulsa City-County Libraries (Oklahoma) presented "Meet the Author: Wendell Berry" with a black-tie dinner Central Library. Tickets were $150 per person. Berry was the winner of the Tulsa Library Trust's Peggy V. Helmerich Distinguished Author Award. In addition, the Friends held a free public presentation and book signing the day following the dinner.

CHOCOLATE & SPIRITS FESTIVAL

The Lee County Library System (Fort Myers, Florida) hosts an annual "Chocolate & Spirits Festival." For one of the festivals, area restaurants provided samples of chocolate creations including mole, chocolate lava cake, holiday flavored truffles, sea salt dark chocolates, chocolate martinis, chocolate beer, and more. There was live music provided by the Randy Stephens Band and a gift-packed silent auction. Admission was free. The event was sponsored by the Bell Tower Shops, Crü, World of Beer, and the Florida Rep Theatre. Chocolate samples, beverages, and chance drawing tickets were sold at the event for $1 each. Silent auction offerings included tickets to Universal Studios, Harley Davidson motorcycle rentals, theater tickets, beach-front family portrait sessions, massages, and more. Proceeds from the "Chocolate & Spirits Festival" benefited the Southwest Florida Reading Festival, a free community event that showcased the Lee County Library System's programs and resources and promoted reading and literacy.

SPRING FUNDRAISER FEATURES AUTHOR

Wingate University Friends of the Library (North Carolina) holds an annual spring fundraiser. The group's third annual fundraiser featured *New York Times* bestselling author Wiley Cash, a Gaston County native, at Rolling Hills Country Club in Monroe, North Carolina. The evening included a buffet, author talk, and a silent auction. "The Friends of the Library act as a champion of the Ethel K. Smith Library by providing promotional, community and financial support," said Christy Inge, access services manager for the Ethel K. Smith Library. Tickets were $50.

SWEET NIGHT AT THE LIBRARY

Friends of the Loveland Public Library Foundation, Inc. (Colorado) hosts "Sweet Night at the Library." The evening includes food, wine, and dancing to live music. Tickets are $20.

WE LOVE OUR LIBRARY DINNER

Friends of Auburn Library (California) hosts an annual "We Love Our Library" dinner. The evening includes a no-host wine bar, Friends-made appetizers, a silent auction, and dinner with choice of main dish. Tickets are $40.

LOVE YOUR LIBRARY EVENING

The Citrus County Library Advisory Board (Beverly Hills, Florida) presents an annual "Love Your Library" evening around Valentine's Day. One year the event included live music by the Citrus County Jazz Society, wine, catered hors d'oeuvres, a silent auction, and raffles. Tickets, which were $20, included two glasses of wine and a ticket for the door prize. Additional wine tickets were available for purchase for a small donation. The available wines, from Aspirations Winery in Tampa, included "Well Read Cabernet Sauvignon," "Classic Shelf Chardonnay," and "Novel White Zinfandel." The specially labeled wines were available for order at the event for $14 a bottle. Proceeds benefited the Citrus County Library System through the Citrus County Library Foundation.

5K RACE FOR THE LIBRARY

The Graduate Student Senate sponsors an annual "Love Your Libraries" 5K Race to benefit the University of Tennessee, Knoxville Libraries. The Graduate Student Senate hosted its first race to benefit the UT Libraries on Valentine's Day in 1992. Proceeds from the race assist the libraries in purchasing much-needed electronic resources, books, equipment, and other items critical for student success at the University of Tennessee. The Knoxville Track Club manages the finish line and compiles race results. An awards ceremony follows the race. Awards are given to the top three runners overall, first masters (40+) and first grand masters (50+), male and female, as well as in several age-group categories. The best team (organization with most registrants), fastest team, and fastest UT runner (student, faculty, or staff) are also recognized. The registration fee for individual pre-registrants is $20, or $15 per person for teams of four or more. Registration is $25 per person the day of the race.

CARNEGIE LIBRARY TROLLEY TOUR

The Friends of the Free Library of Philadelphia (Pennsylvania) are presented a Carnegie Library Trolley Tour on a Saturday from 1 to 4 P.M. Participants experienced five of Philadelphia's historic Carnegie libraries, with master architect and preservationist David Traub leading the tour. Tickets cost $30, or $50 for two people.

ST. PADDY'S DAY 5K AND LITTLE LEPRECHAUN DASH

The Friends of Buckley Public Library (Poteau, Oklahoma) held the group's inaugural "St. Paddy's Day 5K and Little Leprechaun Dash." There were 150 registered runners/walkers, each of whom received a custom medal featuring a rendering of the new library. The Tulsa Life Flight crew brought their helicopter for participants and spectators to tour. The group planned to add a 10K to the event next time to increase profits. About $1,200 was raised.

MURDER, MAESTRO, PLEASE!

Walnut Creek Library Foundation (California) hosted a "Murder, Maestro, Please!" murder mystery event at the library. Several local celebrity "suspects" were featured, including news anchor Dan Ashley, former mayor

Sue Rainey, and actress Kerri Shawn. Tickets were $45 and included wine and desserts.

FIVE Bs CAMPAIGN

The Friends of the Georgetown County Library (Waccamaw, South Carolina) launched a new fundraising campaign at the group's book sale. The "Five Bs" campaign was aimed at raising funds for books, bytes, bricks, bushes, and benches for the new library. Donors could specify which "B" they wished to finance. Friends and library supporters hoped to raise $130,000 for library enhancements.

TINY BUT MIGHTY GALA

The Friends of the Jamesburg Public Library (New Jersey) held a "Tiny But Mighty" gala at Forsgate Country Club to celebrate 50 years at the Gatzmer Avenue location. The semi-formal dinner dance raised much-needed funds for building improvements. Mystery author Jane Kelly spoke, a basket raffle was held, and dancing ended the evening. More than $10,000 was raised to aid the library in fulfilling its commitment to the community.

MINI GOLF INVITATIONAL

The Friends of the Beardsley and Memorial Library (Winsted, Connecticut) held a mini-golf invitational at R&B Sports World. The goal was to earn money to help refurnish the young adult and children's rooms. The Friends contacted more than 120 local businesses, providing a description of the event, the overall goal, the Friends' mission, and past programs and major purchases for the library. In response, 40 business contributed; 6 businesses donated prizes valued at $115 or more. R&B donated all cash from mini-golf games played during the event to the Friends. The Friends raised $1,820 and won an award from the Friends of Connecticut Libraries.

HISTORICAL MURAL PRINTS AND NOTECARDS

The Friends of the Kansas State University Libraries (Manhattan, Kansas) sold mural prints and notecards of the four historical murals in the Farrell Library, painted in 1934 by David Hicks Overmyer as part of the federal government's Public Works of Art Project. Each mural is 11' × 14', and their subjects symbolize the four major academic pursuits of the institution at the time: science and industry, agriculture and animal husbandry, the arts, and home economics. The Friends funded a three-year restoration of the murals, and they were then photographed by Ed Olson. A framed print of all four murals was available for $225, and notecards were $15 per set. Proceeds from the sale of both benefited the Friends of the K-State Libraries.

GRAND OPENING GALA

Before Central Library opened to the public, the Madison Public Library Foundation (Wisconsin) hosted two fundraising events, offering ticket buyers a preview of the building while supporting the campaign. "Foreword: A Grand Opening Gala," welcomed more than 650 guests for a formal affair, complete with dinner and dancing, and netted more than $117,000 for the new library. "Stacked" brought back artists from the library's closing fundraiser, "Bookless," along with some new faces. Lines snaked around the block as more than 1,500 people waited to enjoy art, music, and drinks into the early morning hours, bringing in more than $17,000 in ticket sales.

PIE SALE

As part of their annual Thanksgiving pie sale, about 20 volunteers with the Friends of Meadowridge Library (Wisconsin) made more than 100 pies. Pies were sold on the Tuesday before Thanksgiving at 10 A.M. for just $10 each. The Friends use proceeds from the pie sale and their annual book and bake sales to support efforts like the "Beyond the Page" campaign to create an endowment fund for all 28 Dane County libraries and Meadowridge's upcoming expansion. "We are a small group, but we work very hard to fill the library's wants and needs," said Jacky Byrnes, Friends group secretary and Meadowridge fundraising campaign committee member. Byrnes is looking forward to the expansion because it will modernize the library and bring a "positive spirit" to the area.

TASTE OF SYLVA

During the local culinary event "Taste of Sylva," folks also sampled a flavor of mountain music and "Luscious Literary Leftovers," like "Deep-Fried Drama," "Marinated Mystery," and "Sizzling Romance," at the Friends

Used Book Store, run by the Friends of the Jackson County Public Library (Sylva, North Carolina). In keeping with the culinary theme, Friends social chair Myrtle Schrader set up a tea party outside the book store and used a silver teapot to collect ticket donations for the Friends' quilt fundraiser. Friends members participated in several other local events and festivals to promote the quilt fundraiser. In all, the Friends raised $3,833 from the quilt fundraiser for the Jackson County Public Library.

STAY HOME AND READ A BOOK BALL

The Library Foundation of Los Angeles (California) presented the 26th annual "Stay Home and Read a Book Ball," a "non-event," on a Friday in February, featuring chair Louise Steinman. Participants were invited to read "in a tent with a flashlight in hand, in the middle seat on an airplane, curled up on a papasan . . ." and suggested attire was "maybe paisley or stripes or polka dots or plaid . . ." Donors could give on levels from $25 to $1,000, and were invited to let others know how they were celebrating via Facebook, Instagram, Flickr, and Twitter (with the hashtag #LFLAStayHome).

ANTIQUES APPRAISAL

The Friends of Cheboygan Area Public Library (CAPL—Michigan) held an Antique Appraisal event in October. The public was invited to bring up to three items for evaluation, at a $10 per item charge. The CAPL also held a Fall Fashion Show. The free event accepted donations for the show, which included models of all sizes.

GREAT GATSBY GALA

The Friends of the Ramsey County Libraries (Roseville, Minnesota) pulled off a great fundraiser—a Gatsby-great fundraiser. Organizers tore a page straight from the Great American Novel and hosted a "Great Gatsby Gala" at the Roseville Library. (Author F. Scott Fitzgerald was born in Saint Paul—less than 10 miles from the Roseville Library venue.) The evening, emceed by Minnesota Public Radio personality Kerri Miller, contained several elements common to Friends fundraisers. Silent and live auctions boasted more than 70 donated entries ranging from one-of-a-kind specialty items, to gift baskets, to fun dining, theater, and sightseeing experiences. The rest of the night was, as the name promised, a real blast from the past. Highlights included Roaring Twenties style dance lessons, a costume contest recognizing most authentic period dress, and a photo booth with Gatsby-era props. Commensurate with the party's Roaring Twenties theme, planners set an ambitious fundraising goal of $20,000. By the end of the night, Ramsey County had met and surpassed that mark, with the live auction alone bringing in upward of $8,000. Attendance was equally impressive, with 200 "flappers" and "fellas" turning out. Afterward, the Friends of the Ramsey County Libraries began planning a second gala.

CANDY STORE IN DECEMBER

The Friends of the Beaver County Pioneer Library (Oklahoma) hosts an annual Candy Store in December. The Friends sell homemade candy including fudge, divinity, peanut brittle, and much more. On display is a large and beautiful gingerbread house that is 100 percent edible. Chances to win the gingerbread house are sold and a drawing is held at the library's annual open house.

GADGET DONATIONS

During one January and February, the Friends (Charleston, South Carolina) conducted a media and gadget donation drive to raise funds for the library. Items such as CDs, DVDs, video games, cameras, iPods, and tablets were collected.

FURRY FRIENDS CALENDAR

The Friends of the L.E. Phillips Memorial Library (Eau Claire, Wisconsin) created a "Furry Friends" calendar for 2015. The calendar, which featured professional photographs of library employees' pets, went on sale in the fall of 2014. The calendars were also be available for purchase at Friends book sales, the library customer service desk, and selected local businesses.

BREW AND CHEW GALA

The Friends of the Etowah Carnegie Library (Tennessee) was formed in 2010 with accessibility in mind. Etowah enjoys a Carnegie library that was 100 years old in 2015. Carnegie felt one should "ascend to knowledge," and thus the library has 20 concrete steps into their facility. An elevator was deemed their most urgent need. In 2014, the Friends held their first major fundraising event—the "Brew and Chew Gala," which began as a beer and BBQ in overalls, but evolved into a catered dinner with a musician, a band, and dancing in a picturesque old barn.

SUPER FRIENDS BOOKPLATE

The Friends of the Long Beach Public Library (California) has a special category called "Super Friends." Those who donate $100 or more to the Friends can have a bookplate placed in an Honor Book to create a lasting memorial for someone they have lost or admire. The library staff selects the book and notifies the Super Friend of the title of the book and where it resides in the system.

TENNIS FUNDRAISER

The Free Library of Philadelphia (Pennsylvania) held a tennis fundraiser at the Germantown Cricket Club during the summer. Attendees were invited to enjoy breakfast and lunch and play with tennis masters on spectacular professional courts. Tickets were $275 per person for the daylong event, which went to support the library.

BANNED BOOKS BASH

The Austin Public Library Friends Foundation (Texas) raises both money and awareness from their annual celebration of Banned Books Week. Each year the group spotlights a handful of literary works once deemed too scandalous, too thought-provoking, too agitating, or too revolutionary to be placed in the hands of readers. Their Banned Books Bash celebrates the freedom to read and the right to create literary work that challenges and interrogates the status quo. Local writing teachers read excerpts from books including *1984, The Absolutely True Diary of a Part-Time Indian, An Abundance of Katherines, The Catcher in the Rye, Cat's Cradle, The Hunger Games, The Satanic Verses, Their Eyes Were Watching God,* and *To Kill a Mockingbird*. Proceeds from the Banned Books Bash benefit the library Foundation's (free!) Badgerdog Creative Writing Workshops for adults at the Austin Public Library.

MAKE, CREATE, INNOVATE!

The Riverside Public Library Foundation's (California) 2015 annual campaign was "Make, Create, Innovate!" This campaign worked to provide learning labs, inclusive of makerspaces (customers read to make something) coding camps (customers read to code new or enhanced computer scripts), and technology enhancements (public computers and/or laptops for libraries that need them).

MONTHLY DONATION ACCEPTANCE VIA CREDIT CARD

The New York Public (New York) is following suit of many nonprofits by allowing donors to make monthly donations taken from the donor's credit card. Donations continue until the donor opts out. This could be a good strategy for Friends groups and Foundations, giving them a better way to plan their year ahead knowing more clearly how much money might be coming in.

FUEL YOUR MIND WITH LOCAL INGENUITY

The Cary Memorial Library Foundation (Lexington, Massachusetts) hosted a day of fun called "Fuel Your Mind with Local Ingenuity," inviting the community to join their Friends and show their love for the library at this festive celebration. This fundraiser included speakers and exhibitors who share a love of creating and a commitment to the community. Attendees heard about how Wilson Farms has extended their growing period with the technology in their greenhouses, participated in hands-on activities, and observed 3D printing with staff from Einstein's Workshop and Empow Studios. Attendees also learned about geocaching, an increasingly popular family activity. They were also able to marvel at the ingenuity of Lexington High School's Robotics Teams.

LET'S FILL THE LIBRARY DIRECTOR'S WISH LIST

The Riverside Public Library Foundation (California) made their fundraising personal with their "Let's Fill Tonya's (library director) Wish List" campaign. A generous pledge from library supporters matched donors' gift to the library—dollar-for-dollar up to $15,000—for each donation to the library made by the end of 2015. The money will fund Director Tonya Kennon's "Wish List"—items she would like the library to be able to offer to patrons, but has no funds as funded for the following for branches: 16 19-inch computer monitors for Casa Blanca ($1,450); books for children, teens, and adults ($1,000); a storytime carpet for Eastside ($1,125); sign holders for Arlanza ($133); book display racks for Arlanza ($1,017), and a DVD display unit for La Sierra.

HOMECOMING BOOK SALE AND SILENT AUCTION

During a book sale and silent auction held during Homecoming Weekend in May, Friends of the (Kettering University, Flint, Michigan) Library and Archives (FOLA) made just under $770 for the two-day event, which also included a 50/50 drawing, Kettering/General Motors historic photographs for a $5 donation, and a bookplate sale. FOLA also teamed up with Kettering University's "Engineers Without Borders" by allowing the group to offer some items in the auction to raise funds for a project that will bring water to a village in Africa.

PROGRAMS

ADULT COLORING NIGHT

The Friends of the Meredith Public Library (New Hampshire) sponsored an Adult Coloring Night—the latest trend in stress busting is coloring for grown-ups. The program was increased from an hour to an hour and a half due to popular demand. The Friends provided numerous coloring sheets to choose from and colored pencils for attendees use. Light refreshments were served and relaxing music was played. This program was for ages 18 and over.

READERS' THEATER

Friends of the MU Libraries, University of Missouri, presented a readers' theater production of *The Defeat of Grandfather Devil*, one of the few pastorals from Mexico that remains intact elements from the 14th and 15th century Spanish versions, at the MU Corner Playhouse. The pastoral was published by Josephine Niggli, an author, teacher, and photographer with roots in Mexico and northern Texas whose writing focused on Mexican folk traditions and plays. The play was found and offered for performance by Bill Fisher, a lawyer in San Antonio who attended the performance, which featured traditional music and was directed by Alex Iben Cahill. Tickets were $20 ($10 for students) to benefit the MU Libraries and guests enjoyed a dessert reception following the performance.

ENGLISH TEA

The Friends of the Kirkwood Public Library (Missouri) hosts an annual English tea. During one of the English teas, Sheila Hwang of Webster University presented "Literary Feasts, from Jane Austen's Day to the Present." Dr. Hwang examined representations of food in Jane Austen's novels and then contextualized it with examples from poetry, short stories, memoirs, and novels from the 19th century and beyond. Admission was free for members, $5 for others. The fee was waived for non-members who join the Friends when registering for or attending the event.

SHERLOCK HOLMES SYMPOSIUM

With the release of *Mr. Holmes* starring Ian McKellen, the Friends of the Allen Public Library (Texas) hosted a Sherlock Holmes symposium. The Friends stated that "for Sherlock-ians, accepting clues at face value can be challenging, but there are times when the facts are fascinating and far from elementary. Symbolizing genius and highly intuitive investigative skills, Sherlock Homes remains a worldwide enduring hero. The recent release of 'Mr. Holmes' is a vivid reminder that the works of A. Conan Doyle as depicted by Sherlock Holmes are hugely popular."

NOT SO QUIET! CONCERT SERIES

The Friends of the St. Louis Public Library (Missouri) held a very jazzy concert for Christmas as part of their "NOT SO QUIET! Concert Series." The rhythm and blues group, Harmonie, delighted music and book lovers alike (the overlap for those two groups is probably very high!).

TEEN CRAFT PROGRAM

The Walnut Creek Library Foundation (California) provided funding for a teen craft program at the library prior to the holidays so those attending could make their own gifts for their friends and families. At the first program, teens were taught to embroider and all materials and a lunch were provided. Later, a party was thrown with hot chocolate and treats with another opportunity for teens to make DIY holiday gifts.

BOOKS AND BARS

With the Friends of the Saint Paul Public Library (Minnesota), moderator Jeff Kamin brings his unique take on a public book club show to Saint Paul every first Tuesday of the month under the title, "Books and Bars." Kamin has taken the suburban book club tradition and put it in a public bar where people's opinions flow freely with a little "liquid courage." Even if you don't like the featured book, he "guarantees a good time at our entertaining discussions."

SELF-GUIDED TOUR THROUGH AUTOMOTIVE MUSEUM

The Friends of the Rochester Hills Public Library (Michigan) hosted a self-guided tour of the Stahls Automotive Museum in Chesterfield Township. The museum features rare autos, car-related accessories from the Depression era, and a number of musical instruments. The tour cost $20 and proceeds were used to fund library programs.

RICH FOOD HERITAGE—EXPLORING THE COOKBOOK COLLECTION

Friends of the University of Wisconsin-Madison Libraries hosted "Wisconsin's Rich Food Heritage: Exploring the Steenbock Library Cookbook Collection" on a Friday in September in two parts. From 5:30 to 7 P.M. in Steenbock Library, attendees browsed the 5,000-plus-volume cookbook collection, watched a cooking demonstration, sampled the results, and met cooks, chefs, local growers, food historians, and foodies. From 7 to 9 P.M., attendees walked across the street to the Ebling Symposium Center in Microbial Sciences to hear a talk by Traci Nathans-Kelly titled "Porcupine Meatballs: Finding History in Community Cookbooks."

WORKS PROGRESS ADMINISTRATION

The Friends of the Allen Public Library (Texas) sponsored a program about the Works Progress Administration (WPA) featuring their state historian. For Depression-weary and despondent Americans, the WPA offered not only employment but also the restoration of dignity. Through the efforts of authors, artists, and construction workers, the American landscape was altered for the enjoyment of millions of people. The program announcement pointed out that Texas artist Frank Klepper's mural can be viewed at the Collin County Historical Museum in McKinney funded by the WPA.

LOCAL FOOD SCENE WRITERS

The Friends of the Hennepin County Library (Minnesota) hosted famed food and wine writer Dara Moskowitz Grumdahl in conversation with three other celebrated authors and trendsetters in the local food scene. The audience was able to take a virtual journey from chicken and vegetable farms to restaurants and family tables—and everywhere in between.

CLIMATE AND DROUGHT-TOLERANT PLANTS

Gardening programs are always popular, and the Walnut Creek Library Foundation (California) knows that their weather can have an effect on plant life. They said, "Whether or not we are in a drought, California receives little to no rain in the summer, which is typical of Mediterranean climates. Come learn about our unique climate, and how plants have adapted to regions with little to no summer rain. A professor from nearby UC-Berkeley's department of landscape architecture will show how these wonderful plants can add color and texture to your landscape design. A drought-tolerant garden need not be a lone cactus in a sea of rocks! You will come away inspired and with a deeper understanding of gardening with limited water." The free gardening program was co-sponsored by the UC Master Gardeners of Contra Costa County.

PROFESSIONAL WRITERS AND STUDENTS

Each spring break, Badgerdog (sponsored by the Austin Public Library Friends Foundation—Texas) offers workshops led by professional writers who introduce students to literary works and techniques, and inspire young writers to author their own fiction, nonfiction, and poetry. The program approaches writing with an appetite for discovery, fun, and creativity, while also challenging young writers to try new things on the page. The Austin Public Library Friends Foundation also sponsors "Writing/Art Workshop for CarePartners." This program is designed for caregivers and their care recipients. Caregivers work with a Badgerdog writer to create poetry, record family stories, and share experiences. At the same time, care recipients work with Mobile Art volunteers to create collages, paintings, sculptures, and more. All participants are published in a beautiful, full-color hardbound anthology. This program is presented in partnership with Mobile Art and AGE of Central Texas, and funded by St. David's Foundation's "Health's Angels."

RIBBON-CUTTING CEREMONIES

On a gorgeous autumn day, the Friends of Chelsea District Library (Michigan), who are members of the Chelsea Area Chamber of Commerce, had a ribbon cutting for two new Little Free Libraries planted in two of the city's parks. The event included members of the Friends; Chelsea District Library staff; the Chamber of Commerce; Paul Snyder, president of Friends of Michigan Libraries; and a representative of the Chelsea Rotary Club, which also supported the libraries' funding. In addition to the community donations, the Friends add new titles, monitor the supply of books, and maintain the quality of the service to the community with regular checks year-round.

LIBRARY STAFF OPEN HOUSE

The Friends of the Berkeley Public Library's Central Library (California) workroom crew held the first-ever Library Staff Open House. They kept the workroom open all day and encouraged library staff to stop by, giving each visitor one free book and at least one homemade cookie. Another attraction was the "free box" of odd items that turn up with book donations—from milk crates to jewelry. More than 40 staff members took advantage of the offer, and library staff and Friends felt this should be an annual event.

ESSAY CONTEST FOR YOUNG PEOPLE

The Friends of the Fairfield County Library (Ridgeway, South Carolina) joined forces with the Fairfield County Arts Council to present a "Rock Around the Clock" essay contest for young people. The topic of the essay was "Fairfield County: Past, Present, and Future," and each of the nine winners was invited to read his or her essay at the recognition ceremony that included invitations to parents and teachers. Each winner was presented with a gift certificate.

GAME NIGHTS

The Friends of the Kettering University Library (Flint, Michigan) sponsor game nights for students throughout the school year. This has become a great way to bring students together for a night of fun and good food. The Friends pay for hoagies, snacks, drinks, and desserts, while the students play board games and even ping-pong, right in the library!

HOLIDAY OPEN HOUSE

The Friends of the New York Public Library (New York) celebrated the holiday season at the library at Fifth Avenue and 42nd Street transformed into a merry winter wonderland for this annual Holiday Open House. Activities for all ages included puppet shows, storytellers, circus acts, and crafts. Special guests included the Grinch, Scrooge, Mother Goose, and Frosty the Snowman. This event was free for all Friends of the Library members.

LITERARY LOVE CONNECTION

The Friends of the Hennepin County Library (Minnesota) held a program they billed as "BookMatch: a New Literary Love Connection." "BookMatch" is a new, fast-paced reading series that unites passionate readers with books from highly eligible authors. This past fall, "BookMatch" showcased six Minnesotan authors and three genres in one hour. Hosted by Heather McElhatton, bestselling author and host of Minneapolis Public Radio's "A Beautiful World," "BookMatch" showcases authors from a variety of genres and backgrounds. It's the literary equivalent of speed dating—think a literary "Love Connection." Authors revealed dark secrets, readers were torn by choices, and free books were distributed.

SNOW TIME TO READ

Friends of the Bemidji Public Library (Minnesota) sponsored a "Snow Time to Read" program during the winter months. Anyone age 16 or older was invited to participate, read, and log titles from young adult or adult books. Books, ebooks, audio books, and e-audio books were all eligible (but not magazines or children's books). Registration and recording titles were done online. Those logging 15 titles received a "Snow Time to Read" mug and were entered into the prize drawing held at the end of the program. Each additional 15 titles logged earned an extra drawing entry.

GREAT DECISIONS 2015

In 2015, the Friends of the Tulsa City-County Library (Oklahoma) hosted "Great Decisions 2015." A kickoff event was held at Hardesty Library in January. "Great Decisions" is a national program sponsored by the Foreign Policy Association, a nonprofit organization dedicated to improving U.S. foreign relations in a constantly changing environment.

Topics for discussion included "Russia and the Near Abroad," "Privacy in the Internet Age," "Sectarianism in the Middle East," "India Changes Course," "U.S. Policy Toward Africa," "Syria's Refugee Crisis," and "Brazil in Metamorphosis."

BIKE ART, CULTURE, AND HISTORY

The Friends & Foundation of the Rochester Public Library (New York) sponsored a program called "Ride It: Art and Bicycles in Rochester." The program was a diverse exploration of bike art, culture, and history, including two panels of historical photos of bicycles/bicyclists that were selected by Central Library's Local History & Genealogy Division. The first panel, "Sidepaths of Monroe County," explored a series of scenic but practical sidepaths-dedicated bicycle lanes that allowed cyclists to safely traverse Rochester and Monroe County throughout the late 19th and early 20th centuries.

POETRY READING

The Foundation of the Tompkins County Public Library (Ithaca, New York) sponsored a program featuring local poet Zee Zahava reading from her book *Cherry Burst Candy Lipstick (and Other Childhood Pleasures)* during National Poetry Month. Zahava is a favorite in Ithaca for many. The program was free and open to the public, but there was a suggested donation of $5 to provide ongoing support for the library.

CENTRAL CONVERSATIONS

The St. Louis Public Library Foundation (Missouri) supports "Central Conversations" on social topics important to their public as determined by a survey of past attendees. Most recently, they hosted "Topical Talk about a Sustainable St. Louis." Other topics have included "Racial Justice in a Post-Ferguson World" and "Education and What Happens After High School." Light refreshments are provided courtesy of Urban Eats Café Central.

SHAKESPEARE SUNDAYS

Friends of the Lucy Robbins Welles Library (Newington, Connecticut) sponsored "Shakespeare Sundays" to mark the 450th anniversary of William Shakespeare's birth. The film series ran for four consecutive Sundays and included four critically acclaimed film adaptations of Shakespeare's plays.

OUTSIDE ART EXHIBIT

The Friends of the Cadillac Wexford Library (Cadillac, Michigan) host an outside art exhibit every year to increase the culture and community services of their library. One year, they featured a New Hampshire artist's installation of "Farfetched," an exhibit of large boulders in unlikely places—trees. Kids especially enjoyed trying to find each one. The Friends have also hosted an exhibit of large, lifelike people created by renowned sculptor Seward Johnson.

FREE FINANCIAL WORKSHOPS

The Walnut Creek Library Foundation (California) presented four free financial workshops during the summer, including "Everything You Wanted to Know about Estate Planning but Were Afraid to Ask." The Foundation noted that an effective estate plan allows your wishes to be carried out while minimizing costs and family conflicts. This course offered a good overview of wills, trusts, powers of attorney, and other essential elements of estate planning. The workshop was presented by Estate Planning attorneys R. Gordon Baker Jr. and Kirsten Howe.

BEYOND THE BOOK SALE FUNDRAISING

The Minnesota Association of Library Friends (MALF) partnered with libraries and Friends of the Library groups to bring a free and timely workshop, "Beyond the Book Sale: The Future of Library Fundraising," to three Minnesota communities. "Beyond the Book Sale" shined a light on the all-important fundraising aspect of Friends work. What can we do, in this current landscape, to raise real funds for our library? How do we take those first steps in a new direction? And, circling back to our roots, what does the future hold in store for the tried-and-true used book sale? Library consultant and former Friends of the Saint Paul (Minnesota) Public Library Executive Director Stu Wilson led three half-day sessions covering these questions and more. Each included an hour-long keynote, during which Wilson briefed attendees on fundraising fundamentals, book sale trends, libraries' increasing need for private support, changing community needs and volunteer demographics, and effective social media tools.

GINGERBREAD HOUSE CONTEST

The Friends of the Santa Clarita Library (California), along with the library, hosted its first Gingerbread House Contest. Participants dropped off their creations on a Friday in early December. Houses were on display the following Saturday and Sunday. Each entry was judged on imagination, construction, uniformity in baking, and overall design. First- through third-place winners, and the People's Choice in each category, were announced at the Valencia Library and at the Literary Arts Festival on Saturday. The categories were kids ages 10 and under, teens ages 11 to 17, adults, families/groups, and professionals.

HOLLYDAZE

The Friends of the Covington Library (Washington) hosted their sixth annual "Hollydaze" celebration at the beginning of the 2013 holiday season. The celebration featured the Float-In Holiday Movie at the Covington Aquatic Center, a pancake breakfast including photos with Santa, the Fruitcake Hurl contest, the Community Tree Lighting, and more.

A LITTLE NOON MUSIC

The Friends of the Handley Regional Library (Winchester, Virgina) bring lunchtime music to the library's auditorium. The program is called "A Little Noon Music." One December program featured Madeline MacNeil, whose goal has always been to bring listeners into the song. She sings and tells the stories of the songs through voice and dulcimer. For this performance, she included a sing-along, as she finds joy in making music with her audience.

ENTERTAINMENT EXCHANGE

The Phoenix Public Library (Arizona), with support from the Friends of the Phoenix Public Library and Bookmans Entertainment Exchange, hosted Storyfest. There was a book giveaway to the first 500 children in attendance, made possible by Kids Need to Read. The Arizona Science Center was featured, along with a story science lab, a photo booth, rocket rides, photos with Curious George, a raffle to win a Kindle Fire, and memberships to local museums.

LITERARY SPEED DATING

Walnut Creek Library Foundation (California) hosted a Literary Speed Dating event on a Monday in February from 6:30 to 8 P.M. Singles in their 20s and 30s were invited to come and bring a book they loved, hated, or just recently read as an icebreaker.

FIRST TUESDAY WITH FRIENDS

The Onaway Friends of the Presque Isle District Library (Onaway, Michigan) host a very popular "First Tuesday with Friends" program series. Programs are free, suitable for all ages, and held at the Onaway Historical Courthouse. Special guests from across Michigan are featured in presentations on a variety of interests.

DESSERTS WITH STORYBOOK CHARACTERS

The Friends of the Lucy Robbins Welles Library (Newington, Connecticut) partnered with the Newington Children's Theatre Company to present "Desserts Ever After: Dessert with Storybook Characters." Guests were greeted by members of the Theatre Company portraying the Cat in the Hat, Rapunzel, Cinderella and her Fairy Godmother, Snow White, Belle, Harry Potter, Spiderman, Little Red Riding Hood, and Dora the Explorer. Guests could photograph children with their favorite characters, and children collected the characters' signatures in autograph books provided. Locally made ice cream was served.

PROGRAMS FOR SENIORS

The Friends of Miramar Library (Florida) hosted two very informative programs for seniors. The first was a presentation and two follow-up, hands-on workshops on "Healthy Aging Resources on the Web for Seniors and Caregivers" in February. A presentation on safe and secure health-related websites was followed by a panel discussion on "Conversations with Your Doctor, Health Aging/Healthy Lifestyles, Healthy Aging from a Nursing Perspective, and Tips for Caregivers of Senior Adults." This was accompanied by a Health Expo, including local hospitals, county agencies, nonprofit agencies, and caregiver technology agencies, all invested in healthy aging for seniors. It was so well received that a second program for seniors held in September, focused on senior health insurance options, and was very timely as the new Health Insurance Marketplace was soon to open. Representatives from AARP, county health agencies, nonprofit agencies, and others participated as speakers. This, too, was well attended, and in total, the two programs drew almost 200 people to the library; some of whom stated they "didn't know there was a library here." The programs did so well that the Friends planned yet a third in the series for seniors—"Estate Planning for Seniors and End of Life Decisions."

BOOKS SANDWICHED IN

Having trouble getting big-name authors to your library? The Tulsa City-County Library (Oklahoma) has a great way to present well-known authors and encourage the reading of their books. "Books Sandwiched In" is a noon-time, bring-your-own-lunch program that features well-read members of the community reviewing popular titles. Titles reviewed include *Big Data: A Revolution That Will Transform How We Live, Work and Think* by Viktor Mayer-Schonberger and Kenneth Cukier, *Gone Girl* by Gillian Flynn, and "A Kazuo Ishiguro Sampler." Reviewers include such professionals as the director of communications for Oklahoma University-Tulsa; the H.G. Barnard Chair of Western American History, University of Tulsa; the district judge, 14th Judicial District, State of Oklahoma, and a judge from the Oklahoma Court of Civil Appeals.

AN EVENING OF POETRY

The Friends of the Auburn Library (California) held "An Evening of Poetry" at the library. The event featured an open mic for poets and lovers of poetry. Poets, lovers of poetry, and those interested in listening to poetry enjoyed a wonderful evening where appetizers, wine, and Pellegrino were served.

GAME NIGHT FOR STUDENTS

The Friends of the Library and Archives at Kettering University (Flint, Michigan) hosted the "A-Section Gaming Night" with more than 50 students. The students were treated to beverages, snacks, and submarine sandwiches. They also enjoyed playing video games, card games, and board games with the Kettering Gaming Society, as well as ping-pong. The students were also treated to a new Lego set, but leave it to the mechanical engineering students—they put it together in about 25 minutes!

CONNECT TO CREATIVITY TEEN ART SHOW

The Toledo-Lucas County Public Library (Toledo, Ohio) hosts an annual "Connect to Creativity Teen Art Show" in the spring. The show features drawings, paintings, and sculpture made by more than 100 local teen artists in grades 6 through 12. "Connect to Creativity" gives local teens the opportunity to present their artwork in a venue where it can be seen and praised by their families and the community. The show was originally the idea of the library's Teen Advisory Board and is meant to highlight positive things area teens are doing. A public reception is held at the end of the show, after which students take their artwork home. The artwork displayed is obtained thanks to art teachers in the community who gather and submit their students' work.

ST. PATRICK'S DAY TEA FOR CHILDREN

The Friends of the Walnut Creek Library (California) hosted a St. Patrick's Day Tea for children ages 5 to 11. Attendees learned how to make a proper cup of tea; enjoyed it with soda bread, Irish butter, and a recipe from Bewley's (Ireland's oldest tea house); and discovered how giant Finn MacCoul was saved by a cup of tea.

MAKING MEMORIES—KIDS COOK!

The Newport Beach Public Library Foundation (California) hosted "Making Memories—Kids Cook!," a series of cooking classes for children ages 5 to 12 (accompanied by an adult). "Cooking 101" with chef Zov Karmadian was held in the library's Friends room. "Artisan Pizza Making" at Le Pain Quotidien was held during two hour-and-a-half sessions. "Sensational Salads" with restaurateur Britta Pulliam was held in the library's Friends room. Programs were $25 to $35 per child.

BORN LEARNING TRAILS

The Friends of the Brown County Library (Green Bay, Wisconsin) partnered with community partners such as the United Way to create "Born Learning Trails" at their Central and Southwest libraries, with signs in English and Spanish. They are designed to help adults interact with children to boost language and literacy development, and to help caregivers understand how to best support early learning in everyday moments.

BACH TO BOOKS

The Friends of the Allen Public Library (Texas) sponsor a monthly program that explores different cultures through a celebration of music and books called "Bach to Books." During one program, they featured "2000 Ballet Folklórico" and invited guests to delight in the colorful and exciting music and dance traditions from south of the border. Sporting vibrant traditional outfits, "2000 Ballet Folklórico" presented authentic indigenous and folkloric dance traditions. The result was a lively and passionate rendition of Mexican heritage, both past and present.

LIBRARIES AND MUSEUM PARTNERSHIP

Libraries and Friends groups across California are working with Discover & Go, a nationally recognized partnership between libraries and museums that offers library cardholders from every community, age group, and economic background instant online access to free and low-cost tickets to world-class museums, theaters, aquariums, zoos, and science centers. The program allows cultural venues to reach out to people who haven't visited them or don't know about them, to libraries to bridge the gap between books and hands-on cultural experience, and to the public to explore fun cultural opportunities they might have otherwise been unable to. Library cardholders can browse for tickets online by date or by venue. Once they make a reservation, they can print their tickets, plan their trip using www.511.org, and link to a recommended reading list.

CHILDREN'S ART CALENDAR

The Friends of the Redwood Libraries (Eureka, California) host a children's art calendar each year. Children are encouraged to send in their original artwork for a committee of 6 volunteers to select 12 winners. Every effort is made to select at least one piece of art in every age group for a spot on the calendar, as well as choosing a mix of boys and girls. But in the end, the art comes first. All entries are posted on the Friends' website, and many are made into bookmarks and signage.

CROSSWORD TOURNAMENT

Friends of the Saint Paul Public Library (Minnesota) hold an annual Minnesota Crossword Tournament in June. Solvers in each of three brackets—Amateur, Expert, and Teams (of up to four players)—tackle original crossword puzzles created and edited especially for this tournament. Scoring is based on accuracy and speed. Solvers with the highest combined scores from the first three rounds move on to the finals, with championship puzzles solved in front of the crowd. Spectators are provided copies of the puzzles to play along. Those who aren't able to attend can get puzzle packs for just $5 after the event.

ADULT LITERACY CLASSES

The Friends of the Cadillac Wexford Public Library (Cadillac, Michigan) provides adult literacy classes for those 18 or over. Whether an adult new learner, a new English speaker, or someone who would like to learn to read and write better, the Friends offer special tutoring. While promoting this program, they also ask others to volunteer as tutors.

BAND GALA

The Friends of the K-State Libraries (Kansas State University, Manhattan, Kansas) hosts an annual gala in the fall. One gala included a performance of "Hale Sousa" by members of the K-State bands. Decorative efforts resulted in an array of band instruments and historical band uniforms on loan for the night from Glenn's Music, Manhattan High School, Junction City High School, the Junction City Little Theater, K-State Alumni Association, and the Historic Costume and Textile Museum. Also on display were archival items and maps detailing John Philip Sousa's various travels, including his visits to Manhattan. Reactions to the gala were very positive. Rita Keating, attending the gala for the first time, remarked, "We had always heard how nice the library gala was, but with fall being such a busy time of year, he had just never made the effort to attend. However, after enjoying the evening so much in such a beautiful venue as the Great Room, we will definitely try to attend in the future." Dean Lori Goetsch concurred, "We're always appreciative of the Friends, but the gala is a particularly entertaining reminder of their support. This year's event was great, and we're excited that it will help support growth of our music collection."

A NIGHT WITH AN AWARD-WINNING AUTHOR

The College of Charleston's Friends of the Library (South Carolina) hosted National Book Award Winner and Lowcountry historian Edward Ball in a discussion of his book *The Inventor and the Tycoon: A Gilded Age Murder and the Birth of Motion Pictures*, at the college's School of Sciences and Mathematics Auditorium. In *The Inventor and the Tycoon*, Ball documents the odd partnership between photographer Eadweard Muybridge and railroad tycoon Leland Stanford. Set against a backdrop of murder and gilded-age excess, *The Inventor and the Tycoon* transports readers back to the dawn of the visual media age. Ball's discussion of *The Inventor and the Tycoon* was part of the Friends of the Library's "Addlestone Authors' Series," an initiative dedicated to promoting local and regional authors and publishers to the Charleston community and beyond.

ADULT SUMMER READING

The Friends of the L.E. Phillips Memorial Library (Eau Claire, Wisconsin) sponsor an adult summer reading program. One year, the program was "Spin to Win: Wheel of Reading." Those who registered received "spin cards" to record their reading, which they could return to the library to spin the wheel to win prizes, books, or an extra chance to enter their name in the weekly drawing for a book of their choice. Grand-prize drawings took place at the end of the program.

READERS AND WRITERS MEET

The Arapahoe Library District (Englewood, Colorado) hosted "Inside the Book: Where Readers and Writers Meet," a variety of programs for children, teens, and adults throughout October. The event featured author open houses, meet-and-greets, book clubs, writing workshops, and more. Children wrote and illustrated their own books, and teens learned how to illustrate a story using various techniques and mediums. Adults learned folk and historical tales, presented by a Spellbinders storyteller.

A CHRONOLOGICAL HISTORY OF THE LIBRARY

For the 20th anniversaries of both the Covington Library (Washington) and the Friends of Covington Library, the Friends and the library worked with HistoryLink (www.historylink.org) to create a chronological history of the library, the Friends, and the special partnership of the two over the past two decades. The Friends invited the public to share any news clippings, photos, or special memories.

A PORTRAYAL OF CHARLES LINDBERGH

The Friends of the Fairfield County Library (Winnsboro, South Carolina) held its fall meeting during National Friends of Libraries Week. Dr. Joseph T. Stukes, professor and chair of the Francis Marion history department from 1974–1996, entertained the Friends with a portrayal of Charles Lindbergh.

ALEXANDER MCCALL SMITH AT THE LIBRARY

Loveland Loves to Read and the Friends of the Loveland Public Library (Colorado) brought Alexander McCall Smith to Loveland for their annual author event. More than 800 fans of *The No. 1 Ladies' Detective Agency* and his other books filled Roberta Price Auditorium for the author event.

EXPLORING OUR STORIES

Friends of the Cheatham County Public Libraries teamed up with the County Library (Ashland City, Tennessee), Museum, and the Historical and Genealogical Association to sponsor "Exploring Our Stories" at the library. The idea was formulated by the president of the Friends and the county historian as a way of bringing people into the library as well as the museum (located on the bottom floor of the library building). Friends served as tour guides and provided refreshments for the event. Members of the historical society appeared in Revolutionary and Civil War uniforms. Genealogist Mark Lowe was a featured speaker, and their attractions included a Friends book sale, storytime for children, library card sign-up, and a membership drive for both the Friends and the historical association.

SPRING INTO RESEARCH

The Friends of University Libraries (Western Michigan University, Kalamazoo) was among the supporters of "Spring into Research" at the Dwight B. Waldo Library. Students were invited to this drop-in session—which included tropical refreshments—where they received help through all or part of the process of a research project by librarians, Writing Center staff, and other experts. Help was available on narrowing/defining a topic, finding reliable and/or scholarly information, organizing paper format, and appropriately citing sources. Participants were asked to bring a hard copy of the research assignment to one-on-one consultations.

HOLIDAY MOVIE EVENT

The Friends of the Salinas Public Library (California) sponsored a holiday movie event. One hundred fifty children and adults showed up to watch two showings of *The Polar Express* and eat popcorn. At the end of the film, each child was given a small gift bag containing a *Polar Express* activity book and crayons, *Polar Express* bookmark (purchased from the ALA Store), and holiday stickers.

ANNUAL AUTHOR DINNER

The Friends of the Old Dominion University Libraries (Norfolk, Virginia) hosts an annual "Author Dinner." One year, the featured speaker was Craig L. Symonds, professor emeritus at the United States Naval Academy. Symonds taught naval history and civil war history for 30 years at the United States Naval Academy. He is the author of 12 books. He served as chief historian of the USS Monitor Center at the Mariners' Museum in Newport News, Virginia, overseeing the opening and promotion of that exhibit. The "Author Dinner" event also included the presentation of the Friends of Libraries Outstanding Achievement Award to a faculty member, and a silent auction.

HEALTH, WEALTH, HAPPINESS, AND HUMOR

Friends of the Brookfield Library (Connecticut) was one of several sponsors of "Health, Wealth, Happiness, and Humor: A Four-Part Series Especially for Women." The four sessions were "Why Women's Health Matters" (with keynote speaker former Gov. Jodi Rell), "Financial Wisdom for Women," "Aging in Place," and "There's Still Life After Sixty."

SCRABBLE TOURNAMENT

Friends of the Cadillac Wexford Public Library (Cadillac, Michigan) sponsored a Scrabble Tournament. A $5 entry fee included lunch and two sessions of Scrabble games. Three winners took home cash prizes of $30, $20, and $10.

FLASH PLAYS

The University of Southern California Libraries (Los Angeles) collaborated with USC School of Dramatic Arts professor Oliver Mayer to showcase the essential role of libraries in discovery and the creative arts through a series of flash plays. The original plays—short, one-act pieces written by Dramatic Arts students, faculty, and alumni—appeared spontaneously across campus. "Through immediate, meaningful pieces of dramatic art, this project will underscore the libraries' contribution to writing, performance, and all modes of creativity on campus," said Catherine Quinlan, dean of the USC Libraries. "One of the most rewarding kinds of discovery that our libraries make possible is discovery through creativity, and I know these plays will highlight that process in unexpected and entertaining ways for our community." The flash plays joined several other library initiatives that united disciplines and encouraged inventive use of the libraries in artistic endeavors. The USC Libraries Wonderland Award awarded five prizes to its second largest set of entrants ever. In the Doheny Memorial Library lobby, an exhibition of a giant origami fractal inspired and informed by library collections and built by 300 USC community members, continued through commencement. "As I've worked with Dean Quinlan and engaged more and more with the libraries, it's become obvious that our libraries are ideal partners for a project like this," said Oliver Mayer, professor of dramatic arts. "Our surprising, mini performances will occur in public areas on campus. Sometimes they'll include a celebrity actor, or a special guest writer will compose the plays. The idea is to have fun while spreading the word about the incredible resources that the USC Libraries bring to our artists and scholars. And this is only the beginning." Jonathan Munoz-Proulx, a graduate of the USC School of Dramatic Arts, directed the first flash play in the series near Doheny Memorial Library.

"WHAT DID YOU DISCOVER AT THE LIBRARY?" CONTEST

For its first student video contest, the Friends of the University of Minnesota Libraries (Minneapolis) asked students to tell what they've discovered at the libraries. Sixty students on fourteen teams entered for a chance to win an iPad. The panel of judges—which included Milton Chen from George Lucas Educational Foundation, Amy Matthews from the DIY and HGTV networks, and Karen Gibbs from the educational programs division at *National Geographic*—were impressed with the enthusiasm and the overall quality of the videos. The winning videos, "Through the Halls" and "It All Starts at the Library," can be viewed along with all submissions at http://z.umn.edu/folvideos.

SOULFUL STORY—HISTORICAL CONTRIBUTIONS OF AFRICAN AMERICANS

Lawton Public Library (Oklahoma) hosts an annual "Soulful Story." The Soulful Story initiative began with the Oklahoma Tourism Department's efforts to showcase the historical contributions of African Americans across the state. One year, Wallace Moore Sr. portrayed Bass Reeves, a deputy U.S. Marshal from the area. The "Soulful Story" event also featured a barbecue dinner catered by John & Cook's. The event was attended by 139 people and was sponsored by the library and the Friends of the Library.

CELEBRATING THE CITY'S ANNIVERSARY

The Cary Library (Lexington, Massachusetts) celebrated Lexington's 300th anniversary with a month-long art exhibit featuring work by 25 artists in a range of media. Awards were presented for most distinctive, most in keeping with the theme, best in show, people's choice, and honorable mention. The month-long celebration included a reception for the artists. A percentage of sales from the show went to the Cary Library Memorial Foundation to support library programs.

THE FUTURE OF LIBRARIES

Following a social gathering, business meeting, and awards session during the annual meeting of the Friends of the Brown County Library (Green Bay, Wisconsin), the group presented guest speaker Garry Golden, who discussed "Foresight and the Future of Libraries." Golden is a professionally trained futurist who speaks on issues shaping business and society in the 21st century. He holds a bachelor's degree in library studies from the University of Wisconsin at Madison.

CELEBRATION OF LOCAL AUTHORS AND ILLUSTRATORS

The Friends of the Colleton County Memorial Library (Walterboro, South Carolina) sponsored the library's first "Celebration of Colleton County Authors and Illustrators." A dozen authors and illustrators presented a short talk on their works, answered questions, and donated a portion of the book sale proceeds to support the library. Door prizes and gifts were awarded at the end of the celebration.

TEEN FRIENDS OF THE LIBRARY

Vinita Public Library (Oklahoma) has a Youth Friends group with about ten active youth (middle school through high school). The teens assist the library in a number of ways, including fundraising to help pay for new furniture in the children's area, helping to set up for the book sale, and assisting with refreshments at library functions. The teens come to the library right after school and are very enthusiastic. They help with displays and decorating and, importantly, they help promote the library to their peers.

LIBRARY SCHOOL WRITING COMPETITION

For several years, the Friends of Balmain Libraries (New South Wales, Australia) have hosted a "Library School Writing Competition" for children in grades five and six from all local primary schools. One year, the students were required to enter an original short story (800 words) and include in it two key words: "writing" and "story." They could also submit an original poem about an object that was special to them or their families. First prize was a book voucher from the local bookstore and a deposit of $100 in a bank account. Competing schools also received a $250 book voucher for the libraries.

BOOTS & BOOKS WEEKLONG FESTIVAL

"Boots & Books" was the name given to the West Texas Book Festival (Abilene, Texas). The weeklong event used the Western theme to feature writers of the genre, including Dean Smith (*Cowboy Stuntman*), who talked about his book and his career as a stuntman in Westerns. Also featured were local cookbook authors and a special book signing by Kay Bailey Hutchison.

BANNED BOOKS WEEK

For Banned Books Week, Friends of the Kirkwood Public Library (Missouri) sponsored a free presentation by local book and theater reviewer Bob Boyd titled "The Censor's Dilemma: Keeping Society Safe for Misfits,

Dissenters, and the Outright Weird." At the event, the Friends sold used books that have a history of being banned or challenged at the event.

MEMORIAL LECTURE SERIES

Celebrating National Friends of Libraries Week and honoring the late civic leader Norman Gill, the North Shore Library (Glendale, Wisconsin) presented its annual Norman Gill Memorial Lecture. The program featured noted local historians Paul Geenen and Bobby Tanzilo. The event, sponsored by the Friends of the North Shore Library, was free and open to the public. Geenen is an entrepreneur, a community activist, an author, and a grandfather of eight. Tanzilo is managing editor at OnMilwaukee.com, and his work has appeared in the *Chicago Tribune, Milwaukee Sentinel, Consumers Digest,* and *Il Monferrato* (Italy). The Gill lectures honor the memory of longtime North Shore Library board member Norman Gill, executive director for more than 40 years of the Citizens Governmental Research Bureau (now the Public Policy Forum). An advocate for literacy and reading, Gill died in 2005.

HEALTHY CHOICES

Friends of the Calhoun County Library (Matthews, South Carolina) provided funding to present "Healthy Choices" programs throughout the year, which included a competitive ten-week walking program that attracted 42 participants, and Zumba, yoga, and weight management classes.

THE WONDERFUL WIZARD OF OZ EXHIBIT AND RECEPTION

As part of the touring exhibit "The Wonderful Wizard of Oz," the Friends of the St. Louis Public Library (Missouri) sponsored a reception with Wizard of Oz expert Jane Albright. A Friends reception was held from 6 to 7 P.M., followed by a presentation from 7 to 8:30 P.M. Albright discussed her personal experience as an avid memorabilia collector and promoter of the Wizard of Oz series of books. Admission was free.

FAREWELL TO SUMMER BLOCK PARTY

The Friends of the Saint Paul Public Library (Minnesota) held a "Farewell to Summer" block party in the library's courtyard as part of their "Loud at the Library" series. The free party featured music by Charlie Parr, the Brass

Messengers, and the Poor Nobodys. The event featured a cash bar and food trucks. Those who showed a library card received a free beer from Summit Brewing Company (with a valid 21-plus ID).

PRIDE AND PREJUDICE—A CELEBRATION

The Friends of the Aiken Public Library (South Carolina) funded a series of programs marking the 200th anniversary of the novel *Pride and Prejudice* by Jane Austen. Programs held during May and June included a dramatic presentation by Howard Burnham depicting Jane Austen's brother, Henry; film showings of *Becoming Jane* and *Pride and Prejudice;* and a group discussion of the novel.

DOROTHEA BENTON FRANK AT THE OPERA HOUSE

The Friends of the Newberry County Library (South Carolina) and the Newberry Opera Guild jointly sponsored a book signing, talk, and reception by author Dorothea Benton Frank at the Opera House. More than 200 people attended the ticketed program where Frank discussed her new book. The Friends provided food for the noontime program, and the Opera Guild provided beverages.

POETRY CONTEST FOR MIDDLE SCHOOLS

The Friends of the Georgetown County Library (Waccamaw, South Carolina) sponsor an annual poetry contest for middle schools, garnering hundreds of entries. Five students selected to receive the contest awards read their poetry at a Friends' reception and also receive prizes from local businesses that co-sponsor the contest. Winning compositions are published in the local newspaper.

BOOK FESTIVAL

The Friends of the Auburn Library (California) hold an annual Gold Country Book Festival in May. Local published authors are stationed throughout the library grounds. Professionals in all phases of the creation, production, marketing, and selling of books present workshops. Featured authors cover a wide range of genres, including biography, mystery, nature, history, art, and more. The free event also includes a community storybook and a children's book booth.

CLYDE EDGERTON AT THE LIBRARY

The Friends of the Carlyle Campbell Library (Meredith College, Raleigh, North Carolina) welcomed Clyde Edgerton as the featured speaker at the group's fall dinner. The cost was $20, $18 for Friends, and $10 for student Friends. Edgerton discussed his novel *The Night Train*, an acclaimed story of the South, of race, and of the transforming potential of music. He is the author of ten novels, a memoir, and numerous short stories and essays. Meredith College Archives in the library houses a special collection of Edgerton publications and related materials.

DINNER WITH RARE BOOK AND SPECIAL COLLECTIONS CURATOR

Mark Dimunation, chief of the Rare Book and Special Collections Division at the Library of Congress, was the featured speaker following a Friends of the Library annual dinner (Oberlin College, Ohio). A specialist in 18th- and 19th-century English and American printing, Dimunation is responsible for the largest collection of rare books in North America. The Library of Congress's rare book holdings include George Washington's copy of the U.S. Constitution, the first printed map containing the word America, the Gutenberg Bible, the Bay Psalm Book (the first book printed in what is now the United States), and Thomas Jefferson's handwritten original rough draft of the Declaration of Independence, as well as its first printed copy. Dimunation's visit to Oberlin coincided with an exhibition from the Art Library's own collection of architectural books in Jefferson's library that was prepared in consultation with library staff by students enrolled in a course taught by John Harwood, associate professor of art. While on campus, Dimunation participated in Harwood's class and conducted a master class for faculty on teaching with rare books and special-collection materials.

YOUNG PROFESSIONALS CLUB

The Young Literati, the St. Louis Public Library Foundation's (Missouri) young professionals group, has engaged area professionals with creative and unique events. They host a free, monthly book exchange. Exchanges are held at the Schlafly Tap Room on the second Tuesday of every month at 6 P.M. Attendees bring a book or two to trade while they chat and enjoy beers. The Young Literati group also took to the streets of downtown St. Louis on a literary pub crawl. Participants toured several sites of historical and artistic significance, along with several downtown bars.

ADVOCACY

STATEWIDE FIGHT FOR STATE LIBRARY

Friends of Libraries in Oklahoma (FOLIO) called on all library supporters to fight further cuts to the state library's budget. When the state library had been cut just over 30 percent since 2008, FOLIO wanted to ensure that an additional 10 percent wasn't cut for the coming year. Educating library supporters about how important the state library services are at the local level, they shared the fact that the State Department of Libraries furnishes interlibrary loan, online databases, summer reading program training (including technology and certification classes), assistance with Internet broadband access, assistance with federal grants, website hosting for some public libraries, and so much more. It is critically important for all library supporters and patrons to understand what cuts to state library funding translate into service cuts at the local level.

FOLIO also gave specific instructions of what library advocates can do:

- Attend Legislative Day.
- Invite legislators to library events.
- Write letters to the editor in local newspapers.
- Communicate and energize people in your community.
- Mobilize local Friends and advocates to vote.
- Attend the advocacy workshop hosted by FOLIO.

EMAIL CAMPAIGN

The Friends of the Phoenix Public Library (Arizona) sent an email missive to their members, encouraging them to weigh in support of the proposed 2016–2017 budget, which included an increase to the library's e-materials budget. The email read in part: "While we're grateful that City Council has included any increase to library services, we as library users and supporters know that the real strength of the modern library is in its role as a community center, and that access to literacy resources is of paramount importance. As such, we'll be thanking City Council for the proposed increase to materials that are accessible outside of library hours while reminding them that opening every library every day is still our ultimate goal." They provided their members and supporters with a click-through portal for sending a letter of support directly to the City Council and provided both talking points and a schedule for citywide budget hearings.

EDUCATION AND ADVOCACY COMMITTEE ALERTS

The Friends of the Sacramento Public Library (California) have a Library Education and Advocacy Committee, which sent out advocacy alerts ahead of important budget hearings of the City Council urging all its members and library supporters to attend. To underline the urgency of the request, the committee chair said: "If Measure [X] is not renewed, the library system will lose almost 35 percent of its city funding, which will result in reduced service hours, elimination of early childhood services, and possible closure of libraries within the city."

DEMYSTIFYING LIBRARY LEGISLATIVE DAY

The Friends of the L.E. Phillips Memorial Public Library (Eau Claire, Wisconsin) were strongly encouraged to participate in their state's Library Legislative Day, held in February. Included in their appeal for member participation were quotes from Friends who had participated in the past. They also provided a link for a webinar on "Demystifying Library Legislative Day." The Indianhead Federated Library system and the L.E. Phillips Memorial Library arranged for a bus to take library supporters to the state capital to let legislators know that there is strong citizen support for libraries across the state.

LIBRARY LOVERS UNITE!

The Women's Club of Hollister, First 5, and the Foundation of the Tompkins County Public Library (Ithaca, New York) hosted a "Library Lovers Unite!" photography event, inviting all library lovers to come to the library to get their picture taken. Local photographer Luke Whitlow captured a group photo outside the library. The invitation read, "Library love comes in every shape and size—from kids who've just discovered the thrill of reading by themselves, teens who collaborate on projects after school, professionals who use the library's workforce resources, to seniors who are keeping current with sessions on digital literacy."

AUTHORS AS ADVOCATES

Authors can be powerful spokespeople for libraries. If you have an author or two in your community, you might enlist them to write to your mayor as Judy Blume did in New York City. Her letter, titled, "Are you there, Mayor? It's Me, Judy Blume," said "Librarians are the protectors of intellectual freedom. They are the defenders of books and imagination and thought. They are on the front lines, working every day to improve literacy, to close the digital divide, and to spark creativity in everyone who walks through their doors." You don't need an author as well known as Judy Blume—even local authors have clout. United for Libraries can help you find authors in your area through the Authors for Libraries program. For more information, visit www.authorsforlibraries.org.

TELL YOUR LIBRARY STORY VIDEO COMPILATION

The Boca Raton Public Library's (Florida) multimedia storytelling project "Tell Your Library Story" collected stories from patrons of all ages, former and current staff, volunteers, and others. Dr. Caren Neile presented a video compilation and a live performance based on the stories collected. Admission was free. Those who wanted to tell their story were offered assistance at the writing workshop at the Discover Center of the Downtown Library. Written stories were collected by the library and tweeted to @BocaLibrary.

FACEBOOK ADVOCACY

The editor of the *Berkeley Bookmark* (the newsletter of the Friends of the Berkeley Public Library—California) uses Facebook frequently to engage library users, potential users, and, of course, potential Friends. She says, "Every few days your stalwart newsletter editor steps boldly into the Intermire and posts something on Facebook about the Friends, or books, or bookstores. It can be an interesting quote ('I don't judge people. Until I see their bookshelf.'), sign ('Keep Calm and Read Books'), or photo. I can tell how many Facebook users 'Like' us, and how many view and/or share whatever I've posted." This is an easy and fun way to move your own Friends group online—if you're not there already.

EASY FORM FOR LETTERS TO DECISION-MAKERS

As Mayor de Blasio, Speaker Mark Viverito, and the City Council made decisions about the future of New York, the New York Public Library (NYPL) made available a form on its website to send a letter to the decision-makers asking them to support the library. A digital form was made available and requested "enough city support for the 88 branches in the NYPL network; a renovated central branch library that provides longer hours, more public space, and more resources for children, teachers, job seekers, and more, and capital funding to help update the infrastructure of our library buildings." For every person who signed the letter, the library emailed a personalized bookmark to City Hall to demonstrate just how many people support these critical services.

INFOGRAPHIC ABOUT AMERICA'S LOVE FOR LIBRARIES

Cecil County Public Library (Elkton, Maryland) created an infographic on "What Do Americans Say about Public Libraries?" The infographic, along with a customizable advocacy PowerPoint, can be found at the library's website. The statistics in the infographic are from Pew Research Center reports. The library encourages advocates to customize the resources. It can be used to show elected officials how much Americans value public libraries, while telling them what your library is doing to help the community.

TALKING POINTS FOR ADVOCATES

After devastating cuts to the Roswell Public Library (Georgia), the Friends mounted a campaign to urge their members to take action. As stated in their newsletter, "Now may be the time to stop grumbling and decide to let our Fulton County Commissioners know that you are unhappy with the current library situation. Since they are all up for reelection in May, their hearing may be especially keen." The newsletter went on to tell readers how they could help, including writing one's own letter or copying their sample. Also included were the following talking points:

- Making the library less available to users by restricting hours and cutting staff will have far-reaching, negative consequences.
- Reducing library hours, especially on the weekend, is not good: Working families use the libraries on weekends.
- The decision to close all libraries on the same day each week was ill-conceived and foolish.
    Children benefit greatly from library programs:
    1. Literacy skills are improved by library visits;
    2. Taking a child to the library is one way a parent can offer reinforcement, especially if the parents' skills are weak.
- Circulation is up, computer use is up; we need staff to support this use.
- The lack of physical space at the library is detrimental to the community; even if programs are free, they can't be offered when staffing is inadequate or the building is closed.
- Libraries are important contributors to a well-informed electorate; free access to information is an important feature of a democracy.

STATE SECRETARY HONORED AS SUPPORTER OF THE MONTH

Washington's Secretary of State Sam Reed was honored as Whitman County Library's Supporter of the Month during his visit to the Colfax Library (Washington). Library Director Kristie Kirkpatrick thanked Secretary Reed for his oversight of the Washington State Library, which was at risk of closure before coming under the wing of the Secretary's office. The Washington State Library provides many services to local libraries including the administration of federal funds. One year, Whitman County Library received these funds for the Rural Heritage project, Ask Us 24/7 online librarian service, downloadable audiobooks, statewide databases, continuing education, and more. The state library also provides local libraries with access to valuable consulting and training services. The Board of Trustees and administration of the Whitman County Rural Library District sponsor the Library Supporter award to recognize those individuals and groups that play an irreplaceable role in supporting and supplementing the library's budget and activities.

ADVOCACY AND SUPPORT AWARDS

During one of its annual meetings, Friends of South Carolina Libraries (Florence, South Carolina) presented Beverly Hiller with the John Landrum Advocacy Award. Hiller was nominated by Barry Wingard, president of the Friends of the Florence County Library. The award seeks to recognize individuals whose "advocacy, support, and encouragement have been critical in recognition of the value of library services." Hiller's leadership role in securing funding over a period of years for the Florence County main library building, spearheading the establishment of successful library programs, actively participating as an officer of the Friends organization, as well as her personal contributions to the Florence County Library, were detailed in the nomination letter.

FRIEND OF THE YEAR AWARD

During a Friends of Tennessee Libraries' Trustees and Friends (Chattanooga, Tennessee) luncheon held at the Tennessee Library Association's conference, Friends of the Benton County Library were given the Friend of the Year Award. Friends of the Benton County Library, which serves a community of only 16,000, raised more than $22,000 to prevent the system from losing its affiliation with the state's regional library system when local government failed to honor its Maintenance of Effort contract with the state. Working with state and local officials, using social media, contacting news outlets, and mobilizing local residents to become advocates, the Friends and their community stood up for their library. Fundraisers included a silent auction and a radio-thon. In addition, Larry Hinton, chair of Sumner County Library Board and Portland Area Library Foundation, was awarded Trustee of the Year. During Hinton's tenure on the Sumner County Library Board and Portland Area Foundation, three large libraries were built in the county. An accessible and dedicated advocate, he continues to promote libraries as community assets.

SHOWING UP!

The Citrus County Commissioners held a forum regarding tax changes that would affect all residents and in particular funding for libraries. The Friends of Central Ridge Library (Beverly Hills, Florida), including Friends from the five county libraries, made a strong showing at the forum, speaking to commissioners to let them know that now more than ever, the residents of Citrus County depend on libraries.

TRAVELING TO THE STATE CAPITAL

The Friends of Rowan Public Library Board members (Salisbury, North Carolina) traveled to Raleigh, North Carolina, for Library Legislative Day to tell legislators how important the library is in the community and to ask them to restore needed levels of state aid funding to libraries. Friends Board officers Dale Basinger, Dane Hargrove, and Gavine Pitner attended the Rally for Libraries with library Director Jeff Hall and library Manager Suzanne White. The morning began with a pep rally featuring comments by State Librarian Cal Shepard and Cultural Resources Secretary Linda Carlisle. Later, the Friends Board members spoke with legislators representing Rowan County. The rally, sponsored by the North Carolina Public Library Directors Association, provided storytelling, popcorn, and ice cream to legislators and attendees on the Halifax Mall at the legislative building.

For a free "Power Guide for Successful Advocacy" and lots of examples from winning campaigns, visit ala.org/united/powerguide.

FRIENDS ENGAGE COMMUNITY

These wonderful ideas and work of Friends groups all across the country shows how incredibly valuable they can be. In addition to raising money, they work tirelessly to promote the library and engage community. In recent years, they have begun taking on the role of active library advocates. Friends groups, by their very existence, show the community and campus how valuable the library is to this cohort of volunteers. By their actions, they tell the community and, importantly, community funders that the library is worth supporting—both by tax dollars and by their valuable time.

APPENDIX A

SAMPLE MEMORANDUM OF UNDERSTANDING

Sample Memorandum of Understanding between Friends and Libraries

The following will constitute an operating agreement between the Friends of the Anytown Public Library (Friends) and the Anytown Public Library (Library). It will stand until and unless it is modified by mutual agreement of the Friends executive board and the Anytown Public Library administration. The Friends mission is to raise money and public awareness in the community to support the services and programs of the Library. As a non-profit, 501(c)(3) organization, however, it is a legally distinct entity and is not a part of the Library.

- *The Library* agrees to include the Friends in the long-term planning process to ensure that the Friends are aware of the goals and direction of the Library.
- *The Library* agrees to share with the Friends the library's strategic initiatives at the beginning of each fiscal year and discuss with Friends how their resources and support might help forward these initiatives.
- *The Library* agrees to supply the Friends with a "wish list" each year that indicates the anticipated needs for Friends support.

United for Libraries Tip Sheet #4 "Tools for Trustees." Used with Permission.

The Library agrees to provide the Friends with staff support to assist them with development of the newsletter, mass mailings, meeting coordination, and Friends promotional materials.

The Library agrees to provide public space for Friends membership brochures and promotional materials.

The Library agrees to provide the Friends with space in the Library for book storage and sorting, book sales, and office needs.

The Friends agree to publicly support the Library and its policies.

The Friends agree to include a member from the library's administration as a non-voting presence at all Friends' meetings and to allow room on the agenda for a library report.

The Friends agree that any and all monies raised will be spent exclusively for library programs, services, and other Library defined needs unless otherwise agreed to by both the Friends and the Library.

The Friends agree that the library administration has the final say in accepting or declining any and all gifts made to the library.

The Friends agree to engage in advocacy efforts on behalf of the Library under the guidance of the Library and the Library's Board of Trustees.

The Friends agree that if they cease to actively fundraise and promote the Library, they will disband, allowing for a new Friends group to be established in the future.

APPENDIX B

ADVOCACY CAMPAIGNS
Legal Limits on Spending for Non-Profits

Libraries across the country are benefitting by their outspoken Friends groups. Friends have waged successful campaigns to pass bond issues and referendums and have used the power of their voices to ensure that library's budget isn't reduced or that it is increased sufficiently to enable it to meet the needs of the community.

The following information is based on IRS rules for non-profit 501(c)(3) organizations engaging in lobbying and advocacy and United for Libraries' interpretation of those rules. Is it really okay for Friends groups as non-profit organizations to lobby or advocate on behalf of their library? Happily, the answer is "Yes!"

The IRS recognizes two different kinds of "advocacy." The first is called direct lobbying and it is when the Friends group itself or its members work to influence policy, legislation, bond issues, referenda, or the budget in favor of the library. The IRS allows what they call "an insubstantial amount." Generally speaking, this means a Friends group can spend up to 20% of its yearly expenditures on these activities if their annual expenditures do not exceed $500,000. The formula changes for groups spending more and you can find out more about these formulas in United for Libraries' Friends & Foundations Zone or at the IRS Web site, www.irs.gov (see Chapter Three of Publication 557).

The other type of "advocacy" the IRS calls grassroots lobbying, and this is when a Friends group (or other non-profit) works to get the general

---

United for Libraries Fact Sheet #23 for Friends and Foundations. Used with Permission.

public to become lobbyists on its behalf regarding policy or legislation; for example, calling on the general public to "call the mayor." In this case, the group can spend 25% of the 20% allotted above.

For example, if your group spends $20,000 a year in support of the library, $4,000 can be spent for direct lobbying (20%) and $1,000 can be spent on grassroots lobbying.

Remember, however, that it doesn't have to cost a lot of money to wage a successful advocacy campaign. So much of what Friends do in an advocacy campaign is educating the public about what is at stake . . . and there is no legal limit on spending money to inform or educate. Also, by using your newsletter, writing letters to the editor, lobbying on your website, you are not spending much money at all!

If your Friends group would like to spend more than the "insubstantial" amount allowed, you must apply for a 501(h) by submitting IRS Form 5768 available at www.irs.gov.

So . . . are there any political activities that are strictly forbidden? Again, the answer is yes. Friends groups (or any 501(c)(3) organization) may not advocate, lobby, or engage in grassroots lobbying on behalf of any candidate for office. Other than this restriction, however, the IRS does allow for some activity for non-profits to engage in advocacy.

The Friends & Foundations Zone on the United for Libraries website has more information on Friends and advocacy along with samples about how Friends can advocate for their libraries on a small budget.

APPENDIX C

SPONSORSHIP AND GIFT ACCEPTANCE POLICY

Sample Library Sponsorship Policy and Procedures

The Anytown Public Library (APL) welcomes sponsorship from local business, corporations, families and individuals. The aim of sponsorship is to obtain funding or in-kind support to provide services and equipment that may not otherwise be available. The Board of Trustees of the Anytown Public Library believes that libraries play an essential role in the quality of life of our citizens and in this important function, the library should be supported through public funding. Therefore, sponsorship revenue should only be used to fund optional additional services or new, "start up" services.

Guiding Principles

The following principles will guide the Anytown Public Library in the solicitation and acceptance of gifts, grants or support to enhance or develop library programs and services:

- All gifts, grants and/or support must further the library's mission, goals, objectives and priorities. They must not drive the library's agenda or priorities.
- All gifts, grants and/or support must safeguard equity of access to library services. Sponsorship agreements must not give unfair

---

Norfolk (Virginia) Public Library. Used with Permission.

advantage to, or cause discrimination against, sectors of the community.

All gifts, grants and/or support must protect the principle of intellectual freedom. Sponsors may not direct the selection of collections or require endorsement of products or services.

All gifts, grants and/or support must ensure the confidentiality of user records. The library will not sell or provide access to library records in exchange for gifts or support.

All gifts, grants and/or support must leave open the opportunity for other actual or potential donors to have similar opportunities to provide support to the library.

Gifts of books or other library materials will be accepted in accordance with the terms outlined in the APL Collection Development Policy.

Recognition and Acknowledgement

The library will ensure that each sponsor receives acknowledgement and to the degree that the donor is willing, public recognition. The following guidelines will be used in providing acknowledgement to and recognition of sponsors:

A letter of acknowledgement for gifts of money and in-kind support will be sent to all sponsors and a copy will be placed on file.

Any special recognition agreements will be stipulated in the letter.

Public acknowledgement of sponsorship in the library's promotional materials will normally be restricted to a statement of the sponsor's name and a display of logo. Standards controlling the size format and location of such acknowledgment will be developed by the public information specialist to ensure both consistency and quality of appearance. Such acknowledgement will not take precedence or have prominence over the library's own logo or promotional material.

For gifts and/or sponsorships valued at over $500, the library may submit a press release to local newspapers and/or publish an article regarding the sponsorship in their own newsletter if the sponsor is willing.

Acknowledgement of sponsorship may also take the following forms at the library's discretion:
- Launch of a special program or media campaign to announce the gift.
- Sponsor's name on promotional materials.
- Small standardized plaques may be placed on donated furniture or equipment.
- Library bookplates.
- In all cases, the type and scope of donor recognition required by the donor will be weighed against the benefit to the library.

Approval

All gifts, grants or in-kind support given with special requirements must be approved by the Director of Libraries. The solicitation of gifts, grants or in-kind support by library staff or Friends of the Library and valued at over $500 must receive prior approval of the Director of Libraries.

Authority for Implementation

The library reserves the right to make decisions regarding the implementation of each grant, gift, or offer of in-kind support. Purchasing decisions, including type of equipment, materials, furnishings, and other components of a gift will reside with library management. All details as to design of programs and allocation of resources will also reside with library management.

APPENDIX D

WORKING TOGETHER
Roles and Responsibilities Guidelines

	RESPONSIBILITIES OF		
	LIBRARY DIRECTOR	**LIBRARY BOARD**	**FRIENDS**
General Administrative	Administer daily operation of the library including personnel, collection development, fiscal, physical plant and programmatic functions. Act as advisor to the board and provide support to the Friends and community groups.	Recruit and employ a qualified library director. Maintain an ongoing performance appraisal process for the director in accordance with town charter.	Support quality library service in the community through fund raising, volunteerism, and serving as advocates for the library.
Policy	Apprise library board of need for new policies, as well as policy revisions. Implement the policies of the library as adopted by the library board.	Identify and adopt written policies to govern the operation and program of the library.	Support the policies of the library as adopted by the library board.

Association of Connecticut Library Boards and Friends of Connecticut Libraries. Used with Permission.

Working Together: Roles and Responsibilities Guidelines (Cont.)

	RESPONSIBILITIES OF		
	LIBRARY DIRECTOR	**LIBRARY BOARD**	**FRIENDS**
Planning	Coordinate and implement a strategic plan with library board, Friends, staff, and community.	Ensure that the library has a strategic plan with implementation and evaluation components.	Provide input into the library's strategic plan and support its implementation.
Fiscal	Prepare an annual budget for the library in accordance with town charter.	Seek adequate funds to carry out library operations. Assist in the preparation and presentation of the annual budget in accordance with town charter.	Conduct fund raising to support the library's mission and plans.
Advocacy	Promote the mission of the library within the community. Educate the library board, Friends, and community regarding local, state, and federal issues that impact the library.	Promote the mission of the library within the community. Advocate for the library to legislators.	Promote the mission of the library within the community. Advocate for the library to legislators.
Meetings	Participate in library board and Friends meetings. Ensure that there is a liaison from the board to the Friends and vice versa.	Participate in all board meetings. Appoint a liaison to the Friends Board and become a member of the Friends.	Maintain a liaison to the library board.
Networking	Encourage City Board and Friends to join state and national professional organizations and make them aware of educational opportunities.	Join the Association of Connecticut Library Boards as a resource for policies, operations and advocacy for libraries.	Join the Friends of Connecticut Libraries as a resource to better support the library.

APPENDIX E

GUIDELINES FOR GIVING

Friends work hard throughout the year to raise money for the library. Book sales, special events, and membership dues provide revenues that can greatly enhance the library. Given the non- profit status of Friends, is there a legal guideline for how much a group should or must give to the library each year? The answer is "no." Because government regulations regarding 501(c)(3) organizations cover everything from non-profit Friends' groups to huge charitable organizations such as the Red Cross, it isn't possible to come up with a formula that fits all non-profits' missions.

United for Libraries, however, does provide guidelines for Friends groups that are not also Foundations (those that work to raise large amounts of money through endowments and planned giving opportunities). These guidelines are specifically for groups that raise smaller amounts of money from many people, activities, and events each year.

Based on best practices of Friends groups across the country, United for Libraries recommends that Friends groups divest themselves of approximately 80-100% of the funds they raise each year (minus operating costs) by giving the money to the library. The group might consider holding back 20% of one year's typical budget to cover the costs of operations for a year or two should there be a time of great transition in the group when fundraising isn't possible. Here are the reasons why we recommend these guidelines:

United for Libraries Fact Sheet #22 for Friends and Foundations. Used with Permission.

1. Most people want to give to a Friends group because they want to ensure that their money is going to help the library—not sitting in a bank. They hope to see their gifts used right away to purchase equipment, books and/or develop programs.
2. If community members find that an organization such as the Friends has a large bank account, they are likely to give instead to another non-profit they see as being in greater "need."
3. Most libraries do not have the resources to do all they want to do to serve the community each year and that's where the Friends come in—to raise as much money possible each year to support the library each year for those "extras" that are not normally covered by a library's budget.
4. A Friends group wishing to establish a large "rainy day" fund or endowment fund should consider starting a Foundation whose mission will be to establish a large fund for a specific purpose. See United for Libraries Fact Sheet #16, "How to Organize a Foundation."

Very often, the Friends will ask the library administration to provide them with a wish list and then choose what they want to fund from the list. Of course, if the library administration engages the Friends in a strategic planning discussion each year as United for Libraries recommends, then the Friends will have a much better understanding about what the library needs most and will usually be very happy to help fund those needs.

Exception

There are, of course, times when the library will need large sums of money in the near future for such capital expenditures as computer labs, remodeling, or building support. In this case, the Friends group and the library may agree that Friends will raise funds for these capital needs for several years. When this is the case, Friends should make clear to their members that funds will be saved for a few years to amass the amount needed for a special project.

APPENDIX F

MAKING THE CASE FOR AN ACADEMIC FRIENDS OF THE LIBRARY GROUP

More and more academic libraries are starting Friends groups on campus. Having such groups is a great way to generate more awareness about the library and what it has to offer, create a natural advocacy group, and raise additional funds for the library.

Sometimes, however, the college or university development office turns down requests to start such a group. They may feel that you'd be competing for the same funds and/or donors. They might not see the need for such a group, or they might feel that this is their job—not yours.

It's important, of course, to have the development office's support before establishing a Friends of the Library group. If you have any trouble convincing them, here are a few tips to help you make your case.

1. Friends groups can generate greater awareness about the library and all it has to offer. These groups can provide additional communication points for the library, including newsletters and social networking.
2. Friends groups can assist in an academic library's mission to develop external relations through communications, publications, events, donor cultivation, and stewardship.
3. Friends groups typically raise small amounts of money from many donors. These "small" donors can be shared with the development office for potential large gifts now or later.

United for Libraries Fact Sheet #29 for Friends and Foundations. Used with Permission.

4. Academic Friends provide opportunities for involvement and participation in the work of the organization. Library staff can serve on Friends' committees and use this service as evidence of participation in the mission of the college or university.
5. Staff members who are Friends of the Library can help achieve the library's mission to ensure that personnel convey a consistent message about the library, and engage in their roles as ambassadors in order to expand user awareness of resources, services, and expertise.
6. Friends groups have proved invaluable in helping the library develop programs that, in turn, engage the academic community, and often members of the town or city—another potential source for development by the development office.
7. Friends groups and members have an opportunity to join United for Libraries, providing access to committee service and expansion of peer connections.
8. Parents often visit the library when visiting with prospective students—they know how important the library is. A Friends group can provide parents with a small way to contribute while their students are in college.

APPENDIX G

LIBRARY SUPPORT FOR FRIENDS ACTIVITIES

United for Libraries is often asked if library staff should spend some of their time working with Friends, or if a library should share some of its resources to help a group be successful. Some have even wondered if staff time or library resources spent on Friends is a conflict of interest or a misuse of tax dollars! What we have found is that some of the best and most successful Friends groups do, indeed, receive support from the library. Some larger libraries whose Friends groups raise hundreds of thousands or even millions of dollars actually have a library staff member hired expressly to support the work of the Friends. It's called development! It's hard to argue that it's not in the library's best interest to spend, for example, $2,000 of library time and materials on Friends promotion and development when they get back $25,000 in gifts from the group each year!

Below are some frequently asked questions that can help guide the library in deciding just how much time and materials should be devoted to the Friends' work.

Is there a formula we should follow to know exactly how much library time and how many resources should be spent helping the Friends?

There really isn't any set formula, but some "common sense" rules can guide you. For example, the amount of library support should just be a fraction

---

United for Libraries Fact Sheet #26 for Friends and Foundations. Used with Permission.

of the amount the Friends donate to the library each year. In addition, the amount may vary over time. Often, new Friends groups are created by the library staff or Trustees, and in the first year, this fledgling group will no doubt need a lot of support in terms of planning meetings, promotion, copies, flyers, brochures, and membership recruitment mailings. Once the group is up and running, however, it will be able to operate with less staff time (in meetings, for example) and perhaps in support for flyers and postcards.

Other groups will work more closely with the library by creating joint programs, working on grants together, sharing library and Friends promotional campaigns, or printing a joint newsletter. Staff interaction with Friends may spike significantly depending on circumstances; for example, if the library is trying to pass a bond issue or make the case for a new building and the Friends are on the front lines of promotion.

For every library, the support will vary based on the Friends' needs, the staff's time, and the benefit coming back to the library in terms of annual donations by the Friends.

Are there circumstances under which a library should withhold some level of support?

Certainly if a Friends group is not contributing back to the library on an appreciable and regular basis, the library should discuss with the Friends the level of financial contributions the Friends should make in exchange for staff and library support.

Also, beware of "creep!" A Friends group is an autonomous organization with its own 501(c)(3) status. The group should be self-sustaining to a large degree, and should be running its own organization and planning its own fundraising events. A library staff that pitches in too freely with the work may be lessening the engagement by the group's members, and this is not sustainable over the long term.

Are there other benefits to the library besides money that supporting Friends provides?

Absolutely. Friends are called "Friends" for a reason. The best libraries in the country have tremendous community support. When the library works actively with Friends, it is creating powerful community advocates and promoters. Nobody knows better than a library Friend the importance of the library in the community. The more closely the library and Friends work together, the stronger the message, and the better that message gets out to the community.

United for Libraries strongly recommends that Friends and libraries develop a Memorandum of Understanding (MOU) so that as the players change, the commitment from the library and the Friends stays stable.

For further information on Friends donations and a sample of a MOU, see Fact Sheet #22, "Guidelines for Giving," and Fact Sheet #25, "Sample Memorandum of Understanding."

INDEX

#
5K races, 88–89, 96
501(c)(3) status, 4, 9–10, 43, 59–60, 65, 133, 135–136
501(c)(4) status, 53
990 forms, 46, 60

A
academic libraries
    advocacy and, 2–3, 49–50
    recruiting volunteers for, 34–35
    starting Friends groups in, 9, 13, 14–22
    value of Friends groups in, 15–16, 20–21, 144–145
    See also specific libraries
ACRL Standards for Libraries in Higher Education, 19
administration, responsibilities of, 140–141
adult literacy programs, 116–117
advertising strategies, 54–56
advocacy
    for academic libraries, 2–3, 49–50
    examples of, 126–132
    as Friends' objective, 8, 49–57, 141
    lobbying limits and, 9, 53, 57, 135–136
    in merged models, 41–42
    for public libraries, 2–3, 50–53, 126–132
agreements, operating, 5–7, 133–134
Aiken Public Library, Friends of the, 124
Allen Public Library, Friends of the, 72, 104, 105, 115
American Library Association (ALA), 20, 40
angel trees, 76
antique appraisals, 84, 99

Arapahoe Library District, Friends of the, 75, 80, 81, 117
Arcata Library, Friends of the, 83
art exhibits, 110, 114
Atascocito Historical Society, 82
Auburn Library, Friends of the, 95, 113, 124
auctions, as fundraisers, 86, 87, 103
Austin Public Library Friends Foundation, 101, 106
authors
    as advocates, 128
    programs with, 14, 78, 84–85, 94–95, 106, 108, 116–125
awards, for advocacy, 131

B
Babcock Library, Friends of the, 86
baby boomers, as volunteers, 23–29, 36
"Bach to Books" programs, 115
Badgerdog workshops, 106
bags, sale of, 81, 88
Ball, Edward, 116–117
Balmain Libraries, Friends of the, 122
band galas, 116
Banned Books Week events, 101, 122–123
barbecues, 79–80, 86–87
basketball ticket sales, 90
Beardsley Memorial Library, Friends of the, 97
Beaver County Pioneer Library, Friends of the, 100
Bemidji Public Library, Friends of the, 108
Benton County Library, Friends of the, 131
Bergenfield Library, Friends of the, 81

Berkeley Public Library, Friends of the, 107, 128–129
Berry, Wendell, 94
"Beyond the Book Sale" workshop, 110
"Bling for Books" events, 87
block parties, 123–124
board members
　cooperation between, 39
　dysfunctional Friends and, 64, 66, 67–68
　responsibilities of, 28–30, 140–141
Boca Raton Public Library, 128
book appraisals, 83
book festivals, 122, 124–125
"Book It!" 5K Walk/Run, 88–89
book sales, 38–39, 77, 103, 110
BookMatch programs, 108
bookplates, sale of, 84–85, 101
books, handmade, 72
"Books and Bars" programs, 105
"Books 'n Boil" events, 90
"Books Sandwiched In" programs, 113
"Boots & Books" festival, 122
"Born Learning Trails" programs, 114
bowling events, 82, 93
"Brew and Chew Gala" fundraisers, 100–101
bricks, sale of, 89
brochures, 12–14, 30, 134
Brookfield Library, Friends of the, 119
Brown County Library, Friends of the, 114, 121
Buckley Public Library, Friends of, 96
budget cuts, 61, 126–127, 129–130
budgets, for campaigns, 51, 53
Burbank Public Library, Friends of the, 79
Bureau of Labor Statistics, 36
business discounts, as incentives, 74, 77
buttons, campaign, 54
bylaws, 4, 9–10, 60, 65–66
Byrnes, Jacky, 98

C

Cadillac Wexford Library, Friends of the, 110, 116, 119
calendars, sale of, 100, 115
Calhoun County Library, Friends of the, 123
campaign slogans, 51–52
campaign strategies, 53–57
campus libraries. *See* academic libraries

"Candy Store in December" fundraisers, 100
Carlyle Campbell Library, Friends of the, 125
Carnegie Library Trolley Tours, 96
Cary Memorial Library, 85, 102, 121
Cecil County Public Library, 129
"Central Conversations" programs, 109
chambers of commerce, as resources, 33, 35, 78
Cheatham County Public Libraries, Friends of the, 118
Cheboygan Area Public Library, Friends of, 99
Chelsea District Library, Friends of the, 107
children
　need for library services to, 52–53, 130
　programs for, 84, 112, 114–115, 119, 122
　See also students; teenagers
"Chocolate & Spirits" festivals, 94
chocolate-themed events, 85, 94
Christmas-themed events, 76, 86, 94, 108, 111, 119
Citrus County Library System, 95, 131–132
civic organizations, as resources, 33
college libraries. *See* academic libraries
College of Charleston, Friends of the, 116–117
college student volunteers, 24, 34–35, 36
Colleton County Memorial Library, Friends of the, 121–122
Collingswood Public Library, Friends of the, 88
coloring nights, 103
committees vs. task forces, 8–9, 26–32
communication methods, 19–20, 32, 54–56
community arts events, 80
community engagement, 11–14, 32–35, 54–56, 132, 147–148
community service requirements, 34–35
concerts, 83, 104, 111, 115, 116
"Connect to Creativity" art shows, 114
Connecticut Libraries, Friends of, 140–141
consultants, 45–46, 63
contests
　cooking competitions, 90, 111
　raffles, 73–74, 78, 85, 87–88
　spelling bees, 85

video competitions, 120–121
writing competitions, 107, 122, 124
cookbooks, 79, 105
cooking events, 79–80, 86–87, 90–91, 105, 111, 114
"Cookout for Books" event, 91
Coquitlam Public Library, Friends of, 91
core groups, 4–5, 13–14. *See also* leadership teams
Corporation for National and Community Service, 23, 33
costume jewelry sales, 93–94
coupon booklets, 77
Covington Library, Friends of the, 74–75, 111, 117
craft-themed events, 86, 88, 104
Creating the Customer-Driven Academic Library (Woodward), 19
credit union incentives, 71
crossword tournaments, 115–116

D

data, on volunteer rates, 36
Del Webb Library, Friends of the, 74
deliverables, 11–12, 13
"Desserts Ever After" programs, 112
"Diamonds in the Rough" event, 80
Digital Game Development Summer Camp, 92
digital divide, 2–3, 52
digital media presence, 19, 32, 56, 128–129
Dimunation, Mark, 125
dinner events, 73, 79–80, 89–90, 94–95, 119, 125
"Dinner with Friends" events, 90
direct lobbying, 135–136
disc repair fundraisers, 82
discounts, as incentives, 74, 77
Discover & Go partnership, 115
divorce, from rogue Friends, 67–69
dollar match challenges, 73
donations
    acceptance policies for, 137–139
    of gadgets, 100
    recurring, 63, 76, 93, 102
    through purchases, 81, 92
donor recognition, 138–139
"Don't Come to Tea" campaign, 81
Dover Library, Friends of the, 85
dues, 11–12
dysfunctional Friends, 6, 44–46, 59–69

E

e-cards, sale of, 94
Edgartown Library Foundation, 86–87
Edgerton, Clyde, 125
education-based institutions, as resources, 33–35
Egan, Timothy, 84
Eisner, David, 23
email campaigns, 126–127
English teas, 104
Etowah Carnegie Library, Friends of the, 100–101
"An Evening of Poetry" programs, 113
"An Evening with Friends" gala, 72
events. *See* programs and events
external relations statements, 19

F

Facebook, 19, 32, 56, 128–129
fact sheets
    Guidelines for Giving, 142–143
    Legal Limits on Spending for Non-Profits, 135–136
    Library Support for Friends Activities, 146–148
    Making the Case for an Academic Friends Group, 144–145
    Sample Memorandum of Understanding, 133–134
Fairfield County Library, Friends of the, 107, 118
"Fall Classic" raffles, 87–88
family nights, 84
"Farm to Table" dinners, 89
financial support, as Friends' objective, 8, 15, 20, 141
financial workshops, 110
fitness incentives, 72
"Five Bs" campaign, 97
flash plays, 120
Florence County Library, Friends of the, 90, 131
flyers, 54

FOLA (Friends of the Kettering University Library and Archives), 16–18, 79, 103, 107, 113
FOLIO (Friends of Libraries in Oklahoma), 126
food-themed events, 79–80, 85–87, 90–91, 94, 105, 111, 114
"Foresight and the Future of Libraries" program, 121
"Foreword: A Grand Opening Gala" event, 98
foundations, mergers with, 37–48
founding memberships, 12
Frank, Dorothea Benton, 124
"Frankly, We Love Our Library" events, 86–87
Free Library of Philadelphia, Friends of the, 96, 101
Friend of the Year Award, 131
"Friends & Flags" reception, 82
Friends groups
　advocacy by, 8, 49–57
　aging out of, 23–24, 27, 46, 48, 66–67
　benefits of, 3, 20–21, 75, 144–145, 147–148
　divorcing from, 67–69
　mergers of, 37–48
　problems with, 6, 44–46, 59–69
　roles and responsibilities in, 28–30, 140–141
　starting in academic libraries, 9, 13, 14–22
　starting in public libraries, 3–10
　See also volunteers
Friends groups, specific. *See* names of specific libraries
Friends of College Libraries survey, 15
Friends of Libraries in Oklahoma (FOLIO), 126
"Fuel Your Mind" events, 102
fundraising
　as basis for Friends groups, 3, 20
　examples of, 79–103
　merged Friends groups and, 37, 40, 41–42
　rogue Friends and, 62–63, 68

G

gadget donations, 100
gadget repair fundraisers, 82
gala events, 72, 91, 97–101, 116
game nights, 107, 113
gardening programs, 106
genealogy programs, 118
Georgetown County Library (SC), Friends of the, 80, 97, 124
Georgetown Law Library (DC), 84–85
Georgia Southern University, 72, 89
gift acceptance policies, 61–62, 137–139
Gill, Norman, 123
gingerbread house contests, 111
Gingher, Marianne, 73
goals and objectives, 4–5, 6, 8, 29, 38–39, 137
Goetsch, Lori, 116
"Gold Rush" book fairs, 89
Golden, Garry, 121
golf events, 92, 97
GoodSearch.com, 92
governing boards. *See* board members
grassroots lobbying, 53, 136
"Great Decisions" programs, 108–109
"Great Gatsby Gala" fundraisers, 99–100
grocery purchase donations, 81
Grumdahl, Dara Moskowitz, 106
GuideStar.org, 60, 63
Guntersville Public Library, Friends of the, 77

H

Handley Regional Library, Friends of, 93, 111
handmade books, 72
Hanson, Charles D., 14
Hartington Public Library, Friends of the, 82
"Health, Wealth, Happiness, and Humor" programs, 119
health organizations, as resources, 33
"Healthy Choices" programs, 123
Henderson Libraries, Friends of, 72, 89
Hennepin County Library, Friends of, 74, 81, 106, 108
Henry, Tami, 72

Hiller, Beverly, 131
HistoryLink, 117
holiday-themed events, 76, 86, 94, 108, 111, 119
"Hollydaze" celebrations, 111
Holsenbeck, Howard, 73

I

Ida Long Goodman Memorial Library, Friends of the, 76
incentives, membership, 71–79
"Inside the Book" programs, 117
Internal Revenue Service (IRS), 10, 50, 57, 60, 135–136
Internet access, 2–3, 52
Irwin, Kathy, 16

J

Jackson County Public Library, Friends of the, 99
Jamesburg Public Library, Friends of the, 97
jewelry sales, 93–94

K

Kansas State University Libraries, Friends of the, 97–98, 116
Kennon, Tonya, 102–103
Kershaw County Library, Friends of the, 73
Kettering University Library and Archives, Friends of the, 16–18, 79, 103, 107, 113
Kids Cook! programs, 114
Kids Count campaign, 81
Kirkwood Public Library, Friends of the, 77, 84, 104, 122–123
Kline, Robert, 89–90
Kodak Library, Friends of, 79

L

Lawton Public Library, 121
L.E. Phillips Memorial Public Library, Friends of, 74, 78, 92, 100, 117, 127
leadership teams, 4–5, 6, 8–9, 13–14, 26–31, 35
lecture series, 123
Lee County Library System, 94

legal limits, on nonprofit spending, 9, 53, 57, 135–136
letter writing campaigns, 129
letters to the editor, 52–53, 55
libraries. *See* academic libraries; public libraries
library cards, exclusive, 76–77
library directors
  responsibilities of, 42, 49, 65, 140–141
  rogue Friends and, 61, 62, 65, 69
  success of Friends and, 15, 20
  wish lists of, 6, 102–103, 133, 143
Library Education and Advocacy Committee, 127
Library Legislative Day, 127, 132
"Library Libations" events, 84
"Library Lovers Unite!" campaign, 127–128
library staff
  open houses for, 107
  support from, 146–148
lifetime memberships, 12
Lindbergh, Charles, 118
literacy agencies, support of, 65–66
literacy classes, 116
Literary Speed Dating events, 112
"The Literary Vine" events, 87
"Literary Voices" benefits, 84
Little Free Libraries, 107
"A Little Noon Music" programs, 111
lobbying, 9, 53, 57, 135–136
Long Beach Public Library, Friends of the, 101
Los Angeles, Library Foundation of, 99
"Love Your Library" events, 21, 95
Loveland Public Library Foundation, Friends of the, 78, 84, 95, 118
Lucy Robbins Welles Library, Friends of the, 75, 109, 112

M

Madison Public Library Foundation, 98
"Make, Create, Innovate" campaign, 102
marketing, 19–20, 30, 51–56. *See also* promotional materials
Marshall Public Library, Friends of the, 83
match challenges, 73
Mayer, Oliver, 120

McElhatton, Heather, 108
Meadowridge Library, Friends of, 98
meetings, 6, 10, 25–26, 28, 60–61, 141
membership benefits, 11–12, 13, 75
membership campaigns, 12–14, 28–30, 32–35, 71–79
membership dues, 11–12
memorandums of understanding (MOUs), 5–7, 133–134, 148
memorial lecture series, 123
Memphis Libraries, Friends of the, 91–92
Meredith Public Library, Friends of the, 103
mergers, of Friends and foundations, 37–48
Michalak, Sarah, 73
millennials, as volunteers, 24
miniatures, sale of, 83
mini-golf events, 92, 97
Minnesota Association of Library Friends (MALF), 110
Miramar Library, Friends of the, 112
Mishawaka-Penn-Harris Public Library, Friends of the, 92
mission statements, 7–8, 18, 21, 65–66, 144–145
money management, disagreements over, 6, 60, 61–63
monthly donations, 76, 93, 102
Mother's Day events, 83
Mott Library, Friends of the, 16
Mount Prospect Public Library, 78, 85, 87–88
Mountville Branch Library, Friends of, 93
mural prints, sale of, 97–98
"Murder, Maestro, Please!" event, 96–97
murder mystery events, 82, 93, 96–97
museums, partnerships with, 115
music-themed events, 83, 104, 111, 115, 116
mystery-themed events, 82, 85, 93, 96–97

N

National Association for the Education of Young Children (NAEYC), 52
networking, 20, 141
Nevada County Libraries (CA), Friends of the, 89
New York Public Library (NYPL), 94, 102, 108, 129
Newberry County Library, Friends of the, 124
Newport Beach Public Library Foundation, 76, 89–90, 93, 114
newspapers, marketing in, 54–56
Niggli, Josephine, 103
night-themed events, 84, 91, 95, 103, 107, 113, 116–117
Nolo Press, 10
nonprofit status, 9–10, 44, 59–60, 65, 133, 135–136
Norfolk Public Library, 137
North Shore Library, Friends of the, 123
Northern Illinois University Libraries, Friends of, 83
"Not So Quiet!" concert series, 104

O

Oakleaf, Megan, 15
Oberlin College, 125
Old Dominion University Libraries, Friends of the, 119
Onaway Friends of the Presque Isle Library, 112
open houses, 75, 78, 107, 108
operating agreements, 5–7, 133–134
Orange County Library, Friends of the, 73
Oscar-themed events, 89–90
Overmyer, David Hicks, 97–98

P

parties and galas, 72, 91, 97–101, 116, 123–124
partnerships
    foundations and Friends, 38–40
    literacy, 65
    museums and Friends, 115
Paul, Ryan, 91
Pearson, Peter, 38, 40–43
Peninsula Library, Friends of the, 91
pet memberships, 74–75
Phoenix Public Library, Friends of the, 78, 111, 126–127
pie sales, 98
planning, strategic, 26–30, 50–51, 141, 143
plays, flash, 120
poetry readings, 109
The Polar Express programs, 119

policies
- for advocacy campaigns, 135–136
- for gift acceptance, 61–62, 137–139
- opposition to, 64–65
- responsibilities for, 140

Ponte Vedra Beach Library, Friends of the, 84

"Power Guide for Successful Advocacy," 132

press releases, 13–14, 138–139

Pride and Prejudice programs, 124

problems, with rogue Friends, 6, 44–46, 59–69

programs and events
- with authors, 14, 78, 84–85, 94–95, 106, 108, 116–125
- examples of, 103–126
- food-themed, 79–80, 85–87, 90–91, 94, 105, 111, 114
- murder mysteries, 82, 93, 96–97
- music-themed, 83, 104, 111, 115, 116
- night-themed, 84, 91, 95, 103, 107, 113, 116–117
- parties and galas, 72, 91, 97–101, 116, 123–124
- raffles, 73–74, 78, 85, 87–88
- *See also* specific programs and events

promotional materials, 12–14, 30, 134, 138–139

public awareness and marketing, 19–20, 30–31, 51–56

public libraries
- advocacy and, 1–3, 50–53, 126–132
- operating agreements for, 5–7, 133–134
- recruiting volunteers in, 32–35
- sponsorship policies for, 137–139
- starting Friends groups in, 3–10
- talking points for, 52–53, 129–130
- *See also* specific libraries

public service announcements (PSAs), 55

Q

Quinlan, Catherine, 120
quiz nights, 91

R

races, 5K, 88–89, 96
radio public service announcements (PSAs), 55

raffles, 73–74, 78, 85, 87–88

Ramsey County Libraries, Friends of the, 88–89, 99–100

readers' theater, 103–104

recession-themed incentives, 79

recognition policies, for gifts, 138–139

recruitment campaigns, 12–14, 28–30, 32–35

Redwood Libraries, Friends of the, 115

Reed, John Shelton, 79

Reed, Sam, 130

relationship problems, with rogue Friends, 6, 44–46, 59–69

responsibilities
- of board members, 28–30, 140–141
- of Friends, 140–141
- of library directors, 42, 49, 65, 140–141

retirees, as volunteers, 23–24, 34

Richland County Public Library, Friends of, 87

"Ride It" programs, 109

Rio Rancho Library, Friends of the, 82, 93

Riverside Public Library Foundation, 76, 81, 102–103

"The Road to the Oscars" event, 89–90

Rochester Hills Public Library (MI), Friends of the, 105

Rochester Public Library (NY), Friends of the, 109

rogue Friends, 6, 44–46, 59–69

Roswell Public Library, Friends of the, 129–130

Rowan Public Library, Friends of the, 132

Rubin, Jeff, 47

Rutledge, Jane, 38–40

S

Sacramento Public Library, Friends of the, 127

Salinas Public Library, Friends of the, 119

Sam Houston Regional Library, 82

San Antonio Public Library, 90

Santa Clarita Library, Friends of the, 76–77, 111

schools, as resources, 33–35

Scrabble tournaments, 119

secretive friends, 60–61

seniors, programs for, 112–113

Shakespeare Sundays, 109

Sherlock Holmes symposiums, 104
Sherratt Library, Friends of the, 72, 91
signs and flyers, 54
"Sleuth Soiree" event, 85
slogans, 51–52
Smith, Alexander McCall, 118
"Snow Time to Read" programs, 108
social capital, 19–20
social media, 19, 32, 56, 128–129
Solomon, Laura, 19
"Soulful Story" programs, 121
South Carolina Libraries, Friends of, 131
Southern Utah University (SUU), 72, 91
speakers bureaus, 56
Speedway Public Library, Friends of the, 82
spelling bees, 85
sponsorship policies, 137–139
Spring Hill College Library, Friends of the, 89
St. Louis Public Library, 78, 104, 109, 123, 125–126
St. Paddy's Day 5K, 96
St. Patrick's Day Tea programs, 114
St. Paul Public Library, Friends of the, 38, 40–43, 105, 115–116, 123–124
Stahls Automotive Museum, 105
statistics, on volunteer rates, 36
"Stay Home and Read a Book Ball" fundraiser, 99
Stel, Maria, 47
Stoneham Public Library, Friends of the, 71
Storyfest, 111
strategic planning, 26–30, 50–51, 141, 143
string quartets, 83
students
    programs for, 84–85, 96, 106, 107, 113–114, 120–122, 124
    as volunteers, 24, 34–35, 36, 122
    See also children; teenagers
summer reading programs, 117
"Super Friends" campaign, 101
"Sweet Night at the Library" events, 95
Symonds, Craig L., 119

T

talking points, 52–53, 55–56, 129–130
task forces vs. committees, 8–9, 26–32
"Taste of Sylva" events, 98–99

tax-exempt status, 9–10, 44, 59–60, 65, 133, 135–136
teenagers
    programs for, 53, 92, 104, 114
    as volunteers, 24, 36, 122
    See also students
television public service announcements (PSAs), 55
"Tell Your Library Story" campaign, 128
Tellico Village Library, Friends of the, 86, 90
"Ten for Ten" campaign, 91–92
Tennes*See* Libraries' Trustees and Friends, 131
tennis fundraisers, 101
Texas Libraries & Archives, Friends of, 82
textile fundraisers, 86
theater programs, 82, 103–104, 120
Thomas Crane Public Library, Friends of the, 86
"Tiny But Mighty" gala, 97
Tippecanoe County Public Library, Friends of the, 38–40
Toledo-Lucas County Public Library, 114
Tompkins County Public Library, Foundation of, 109, 127–128
tote bags, sale of, 81, 88
Trinidad Library, Friends of, 83, 87
trustees, 6, 9, 39, 61, 67–68, 134
Tulsa City-County Libraries, 94, 108, 113
Twitter, 19, 32, 56

U

"Unbelievable Chocolate" raffles, 85
"Understanding Social Capital" (Solomon), 19
Union County Library, Friends of the, 80
United for Libraries
    academic Friends and, 19–20, 144–145
    recommendations from, 71, 128, 133–136, 142–148
university libraries. *See* academic libraries
University of Massachusetts-Amherst, 90
University of Minnesota Libraries, Friends of the, 120–121
University of Missouri Libraries, Friends of the, 103–104
University of North Carolina Libraries, 73, 79

University of Southern California Libraries, 120
University of Tennes*See* Libraries, 96
University of Washington Libraries, Friends of the, 84
University of Wisconsin-Madison Libraries, Friends of, 105

V

The Value of Academic Libraries (Oakleaf), 15
values statements, 18
video contests, 120–121
Vinita Public Library, 122
vision statements, 18
The Voice for America's Libraries newsletter, 19
volunteers
    baby boomers as, 23–29, 36
    benefits for, 11–12, 13, 75
    differences among, 25–28
    recruiting of, 12–14, 28–30, 32–35
    statistics on, 36
"A Vote for Murder" event, 93

W

Walnut Creek Library Foundation, 96–97, 104, 106, 110, 112, 114
Warso, Edward, 47
Washington State Library, 130
Waynesboro-Wayne County Library, Friends of the, 87
"We Love NC BBQ @ the Library" event, 79–80
"We Love Our Library" dinners, 95
West Texas Book Festival, 122
Western Michigan University Libraries, 118–119
Westlake Porter Public Library, Friends of, 77, 92
"What Did You Discover at the Library?" contest, 120–121
"What Do Americans Say about Public Libraries?" study, 129
Whitman County Library, 130
wine tastings, 84, 86, 90
Wingate University Friends of the Library, 95
winter holiday events, 76, 86, 94, 108, 111, 119
"Wisconsin's Rich Food Heritage" programs, 105
wish lists, 6, 102–103, 133, 143
Wizard of Oz programs, 123
women volunteers, 23–24
Woodward, Jeannette, 19
Works Progress Administration (WPA), 105
writing contests, 107, 122, 124
writing workshops, 106

Y

yard signs, 54
Young Literati, 125–126